The Official
Obsidian™

Strategies & Secrets™

By DAN IRISH
with HOWARD CUSHNIR

SEGASOFT

ROCKET SCIENCE

SYBEX

SAN FRANCISCO   PARIS   DÜSSELDORF   SOEST

Associate Publisher	GARY MASTERS
Acquisitions Manager	KRISTINE PLACHY
Project Editor	LEE ANN PICKRELL
Production Coordination	LABRECQUE PUBLISHING SERVICES
Developmental Editor	TERRENCE O'DONNELL
Copy Editor	MARK WOODWORTH
Book Design and Production	WILLIAM SALIT DESIGN
Proofreader	MICHELLE KHAZAI
Cover Designer	ARCHER DESIGN

Library of Congress Card Number: 96-72675
ISBN: 0-7821-2073-3

Manufactured in the United States of America

10 9 8 7 6 5 4 3 2

DEDICATION

This book is dedicated to my friends at Rocket Science Games and to all of the hardcore gamers out there who accept the challenge of *Obsidian*.

—Dan Irish

ACKNOWLEDGMENTS

First of all, I would like to express my sincere appreciation to Howard Cushnir, technical editor and one of the three *Obsidian* designers, who invested countless hours in my understanding of this game and in authoring the portions of this guide to which I couldn't do adequate justice. Those portions include all story exposition, the Shrink Raps, the sidebars, the making-of chapter, the Snapshots appendix, the detailed explanations for the Chemistry puzzle, and the Church of the Machine.

And, to my friends at Rocket Science, I admire your dedication to such a monumental and ground-breaking product. Thank you to Richard Booroojian for hiring me and including me with such a talented group of people. Special thanks to Ivan Foong, Will Sudderth, and David Shultz for guiding me through the first versions of *Obsidian*, along with Tony Ciarrocchi. Without your help, this project could not have been accomplished.

Heartfelt gratitude to Matthew Fassberg, the producer of *Obsidian* and his generally juvenile, yet creatively humorous e-mails that kept spirits high in the face of insurmountable odds.

Furthermore, my sincere appreciation to Matt McGinnis, who put up with many late hours and came up with creative additions and insights.

Thanks to Steve Payne and Jim Noonan at SegaSoft for allowing me to work on, and be connected with, one of SegaSoft's best projects.

To Sharon Cornelius, who believed in her students enough to give them the tools they needed to succeed in life and who taught me how to write.

And to Charles Cantua, for always believing and helping me "rejoice in thy youth" (Eccl. 11:9).

TABLE OF CONTENTS

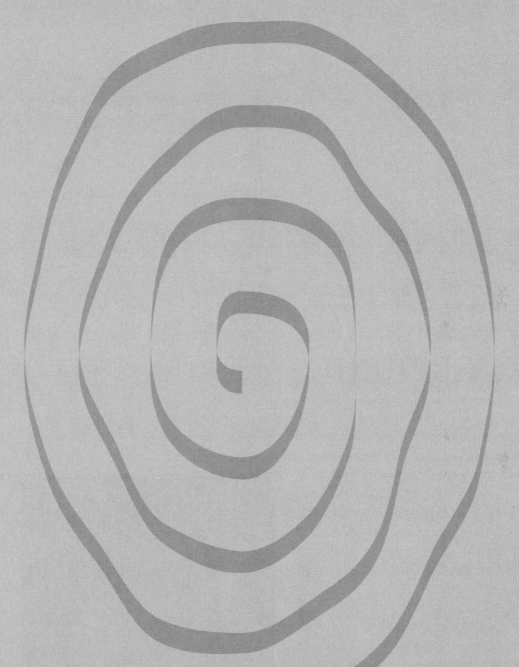

Introduction

"Whatever you can do or dream you can, begin it. For boldness has power, genius and magic in it." GOETHE

Each society looks forward to the future with hope. Although glimmers of hope emerge and can shine for a generation, there are always others who view the future with despair. Alternatively, there are those who live with faith and work toward those glimmers of hope. This is their story.

BACKGROUND

In the 21st century, the world is a very different place than the one we live in now. With new frontiers come new risks. The final frontier we face is not beyond the atmosphere of our planet, but right here, in our own homes and environment—and in what we have created.

After generations of neglect, society has taken a terrible toll on the earth. The environment, once hospitable and able to absorb a certain level of pollution and neglect, can last no longer—given the current volume of pollutants being released every day.

Relaxed pollution restrictions and corporate irresponsibility are the key causes. Air is nearly unbreathable, and sunsets are as red as blood because of all the airborne pollutants. On really hot days, heatstroke and heart failure are commonplace among the elderly and the frail. If nothing is done soon, the atmosphere will be unable to support life on earth.

This dire situation is a direct result of the excesses of the 20th century. While some people heeded the warnings and passed them on from generation to generation, most ignored them. Now is the time to pay the piper and find a fix.

THE CERES PROJECT

By 2066, the earth's atmosphere is on a collision course with total destruction. Once a long-term, low-priority concern, pollution is now at a crisis point and has become a life-or-death issue for everyone. Atmospheric pollution clouds the air people breathe in every nation, and it is not simply restricted to overly populated areas.

The Ceres Project, endorsed by the United Nations, is funded primarily by the United States. That country, which is responsible for a significant portion of the toxins, running a close second to the European Community, agrees to spearhead the effort to fix the environment. Those who still believe that the heightened concern is not valid are overridden, and the U.S. Congress approves and appropriates funds for the Ceres Project. This is the first full application of nanotechnology.

The brainchild of environmental chemist Max Powers and biochemical engineer Lilah Kerlin, the Ceres Project is the only hope for survival—not merely for the nation, but for the world. Commissioned and overseen by the Environmental Protection Agency (the EPA), the Ceres Project will build and release *nanobots* into the atmosphere. With luck, these nanobots will restore the ozone layer, counter the greenhouse effect, and turn toxic fumes into innocuous vapors. To satisfy the calls for caution, the Ceres Project is housed in an orbiting satellite, a very safe distance from the surface of the planet, traveling through the vast coldness of space.

Lilah Kerlin developed the technology for the orbital dispersal system. Her biggest obstacle was overcoming the vast temperature differences and thermodynamic changes from the environment where the nanobots are created—Ceres—to the environment where they are released—Absolute Zero space. Plus, she had to develop and refine the nanobots to withstand massive atmospheric reentry friction and incinerating heat. Although it took years of development, these challenges were eventually overcome.

Max Powers designed and prototyped the nano *factory*. Actually, the factory is a programmable, molecular assembler, or PMA. It is the machine that builds the *machines*.

After a few false starts, some run-ins with the authorities, and miles of red tape, Max and Lilah succeed beyond their wildest dreams. From its home in space, Ceres performs better than expected. With each orbit, the plan is put into action and the results are phenomenal. Clean air is becoming a reality! Not only for the country folk, but also for those in major metropolitan areas, as the nanobots can detect the areas where they are needed most. Finally, both the man on the street and even the bureaucrats in Washington are beginning to breathe easier.

After shepherding Ceres through 100 days of flawless performance, Max and Lilah decide they can relax and take a vacation. They blissfully head for a remote section of forest. Completely free from people, pressure, and the rush of life in the city, they eagerly await the chance to recharge. However, their search for tranquillity leads them to an even more amazing phenomenon.

Just yards from their tent, they discover a piece of shimmering black rock. They notice it, and suspect it to be obsidian, the mineral; but they are unsure, not being rockhounds. The next day on their hike, they notice that the rock has doubled in size. At first, they can't believe it. But, as good scientists, they take measurements and conduct experiments. Their research confirms their suspicions—the rock is growing! Before long the rock, code-named "Obsidian," towers over the surrounding landscape, creating a surreal view from afar.

Over the next couple of days, Max and Lilah watch in wonder as the rock climbs hundreds of feet into the sky. They long for the more sophisticated tools of the outside world to capture this phenomenon for posterity. But, armed with just a camera and their powers of observation, they charge on.

YOUR ADVENTURE

This is where *your* adventure begins. Enter Max and Lilah's world and discover the future for yourself. You join them at their campsite, do some digging, and find clues as to their purpose and the continued operation of Ceres.

You then head toward *Obsidian* and enter its world. Only now can you solve the mysteries that plague Max and Lilah. Look for information about Max's and Lilah's dreams: an infuriating bureaucracy that thwarts its citizens at every turn, a gigantic creature toying with its human prey . . . What is your role here?, you ask yourself. Well, in a few moments it will become clear. But the mysteries will remain and, in fact, cloud the picture even more.

NOTE Every part of *Obsidian*'s diverse and graphically rich environment will help unfold the story. Certain parts are critical to forward progress. Key parts will become apparent fairly easily. After reading through the journal, look and listen. Your first clue is as real as a scream slicing through the silence of the night.

Chapter 1 is where your adventure begins. It involves identifying problems and dealing with them in greater detail. In time, you'll become aware of what to do, but you won't always know what it means. The answer lies in the subconscious. In the end, there is no right or wrong—only the future, as you see it.

HOW THE GAME WORKS

Obsidian, like most graphic adventures, is based on a point-and-click interface. Use the mouse to move the cursor around the screen to determine which items are active and which are just part of the background environment. You can save the game, load a saved game, and return to a paused game using the Esc key. A menu appears when you press Esc, as shown in Figure 1.1. Every element and the environments of *Obsidian* have been created with a purpose. Some are more key to your success than others. Keep your eyes tuned to the details, and soon you'll be able to determine which things merit your focused attention.

HOW TO BEST USE THIS BOOK

The Official Obsidian Strategies & Secrets is a guide that outlines all the elements in the game. The chapters that follow are each devoted to a realm in *Obsidian*. The opening sections in each chapter, the "Shrink Raps," are brief passages that attempt to alter your frame of mind, make you at one with the game, and help set the general ambiance of the realm. If you're playing *Obsidian* and want a little nudge in the right direction, without losing the chance to figure things out for yourself, then *shrink rap* safely to

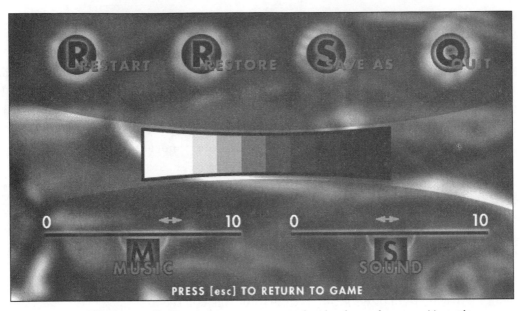

FIGURE 1.1: This menu allows you to save games and to load saved games. Move the cursor to the command on the menu.

your heart's content. The Shrink Rap sections provide an opportunity for you to get the general *feel* of the realm before you try to solve its puzzles on your own.

The balance of each chapter covering the realms provides a straightforward walkthrough that contains more specific hints and tips, maps out a general strategy you can pursue, and offers solutions at the conclusion of each puzzle and realm. If after reading the Shrink Rap sections and undertaking the adventure on your own you become impeded by a particular puzzle, proceed to the walkthrough portion of the chapter for the realm you are in; this will help you get more concrete hints of a solution.

Obsidian is quite challenging, which of course is what makes it so enjoyable to play. However, its complexities and unique approaches to gameplay can challenge even the most adventurous souls. That's where Chapter 7 can be of help. Here you will find *Obsidian*'s cheat codes. You will be well served to proceed with caution, though. The cheats have been structured to provide a single solution to a single puzzle. Use a specific cheat when your frustration has left you desperate. Once you are back on track, go ahead and see if you can complete the realm yourself or with the aid of its walkthrough. Let the cheats be your truly last resort!

Sprinkled liberally throughout this book are various notes and tips, and a warning or two. They are easily distinguished from the body of the text and can also be

Food for Thought

Throughout *Official Obsidian Strategies & Secrets*, you will encounter sidebars like this one. *Obsidian* is that rare gaming experience that tackles complex, adult themes. These themes include dreams, nanotechnology, machine consciousness, and surrealism. While knowing about these topics won't help you solve the puzzles, nor move you forward through the realms, it will vastly enhance your overall experience.

Whenever you come upon a sidebar piece, check it out and see if it piques your interest. If so, read on; if not, go back to the walkthrough.

helpful in desperate situations. If you don't wish to read directly from the walkthrough, and don't want the cheat solutions in Chapter 7, consider using these as a general guide. They will give away only enough to get you unstuck, allowing you to solve the puzzles yourself.

As you immerse yourself in its realms, be aware that there is nothing that can adequately prepare you for the world of *Obsidian*.

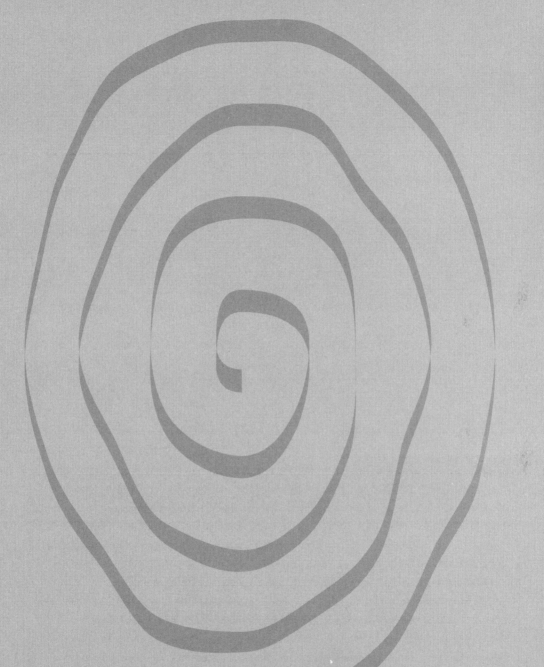

The Forest Realm

O*bsidian*, a dreamlike, first-person adventure through a strange, graphic, techno-organic world, requires you to relinquish your own sense of conventional logic. Within its unique worlds, you must face and understand new laws of very different physical and psychological realities. *Obsidian* offers you both beautiful and eerie dimensions that will challenge you, provoke you, and perhaps illuminate the darkest corners of your imagination. Fittingly, your quest begins deep in The Forest.

Shrink Rap

Who *are* you? Beyond your name, your family history, and your past experiences, what comprises your unique sense of identity? Are you your thoughts? your feelings? your sensations? Some combination of all that? At an early stage of our lives, we become associated with an image—and an idea—of what makes up our "I," or our personality. Much of this comes from the outside world—things said by our parents and siblings and friends. "She's so smart," "he's so full of life," and so on.

At some point, for most of us, there is a moment in time when we begin to question who we really are. Often this happens when we realize how little we actually can control in our moment-to-moment existence. For instance, right this second try to stop thinking—and notice how the thoughts just keep coming in an endless stream. Try to stop breathing, and watch the survival instinct open your mouth and pump air into your lungs.

When we realize that there is not some rigid and unchangeable thing that is "I" or "me," that understanding can cause opposite reactions. On the one hand it can be terrifying,

(Continued on next page)

as if pulling the rug out from under us and creating a sense of atomization. Literally, we seem to blast apart. On the other hand, the lack of a solid ego structure can be empowering, freeing. If we don't have to be *one* thing, then we can become almost *anything*.

AN AWAKENING

Have you ever awakened from a dream and for a moment not realized who or where you were? Did it take a few disorienting moments for the world to fall into place, like coming out of a coma or amnesia, or like waking up from the anesthetic after your wisdom teeth were pulled? This is how to imagine yourself at the beginning of *Obsidian*.

You've found yourself in a forest—but where exactly is the forest, and who precisely are

you? Without the security of some long introductory movie or mission statement, it's up to *you* to decide where to go or what to do. Soon you discover that your choices are not limitless; in fact, they are extremely few. You uncover a hand-held PDA (personal digital assistant) and turn it on. You experience a retinal scan, and you are approved. *Why* are you approved? You keep exploring, still hazy about your identity as if not yet fully awake. You explore because there is nothing else to do.

The more you explore, the more you learn—but the pieces don't seem to fall together. Who is this *Max* you keep hearing about? And who is *Lilah*, and what on earth is *Ceres*?

Perhaps a vague feeling of discomfort assails you, as you continue what can only be described as a massive invasion of someone's privacy. What if the owner of this PDA comes back and finds you snooping? What will you say in your own defense? And what does that ominous black mountain in the distance have to do with any of this?

(Continued on next page)

(Continued from previous page)

When there's nothing left to explore, and things are still not clear, maybe a moment of frustration sets in. But often, when we give up trying so hard, a path appears or an opportunity opens right before us.

When the outside world has defined us too rigidly, it can be the enemy of our progress. But when we have no identity at all, we can turn to the outside world in hopes that it will reflect us back to ourselves.

A sudden scream . . . An image in black crystal . . . A hat on a slab of stone . . . A presentiment of what's about to come . . . And suddenly, all hell breaks loose.

WORLDS WITHIN WORLDS

As a kid, staring out the windows of the schoolroom, were you ever a fifth-grade philosopher? Did you read *Horton Hears a Who?* and trip out on the notion that in every speck of dust there is an entire universe? And what if this whole planet is just a speck on the nose of a dog? "But the universe is *expanding!*" cried a young Woody Allen, unable to cope with the conceptual vertigo.

Worlds within worlds are now shaped before your very eyes. You get the feeling that very small entities are creating something immensely large, something more or less . . . impossible. It occurs to you that the idea of the minuscule is embedded in everything you read about in that PDA. Are you just watching some special effects, or is it instead a scientific breakthrough that makes Albert Einstein look like a young Woody Allen?

Are you dreaming? Are you being dreamed? Did you ever really wake up at all? Is there ever a time when the waking world and the dream world are exactly the same? Are you standing in that moment in time?

IN THE TENT

Obsidian begins in The Forest, where you find yourself literally deep in the woods. Move the mouse to the right until the cursor changes to a right arrow. Click to turn right, and then place the mouse cursor in the center of the screen. The cursor will become a forward arrow, as shown in Figure 2.1. Click to go forward.

As you move forward, you have the opportunity to view Obsidian from afar. After the main title appears, use your cursor to look back down. Then, one click forward will take you all the way through a credit sequence to Max and Lilah's campsite.

FIGURE 2.1: Position the cursor as shown, and click on the center of the screen to walk forward.

As you come to rest after your trek, notice that Max and Lilah's tent is on your left. Move the mouse cursor to the left side of the screen and click. Your view should rotate 90 degrees to the left, and you should be facing the tent, as shown in Figure 2.2. Go ahead and enter it by clicking forward on the center of the screen.

THE PDA

Notice the two sleeping bags. Go ahead and open them.

Inside the sleeping bags, what do you find? The one to the right contains a futuristic personal digital assistant (PDA). Pick it up. When you do, the screen will change so that the PDA takes up your full view. Turn the PDA on by pressing the power button on the right-hand side (see Figure 2.3).

> ## NOTE
> In the tent you can pick up the PDA but nothing else. The cursor identifies which objects you can pick up or use. The diamond-shaped cursor means there is nothing there for you at your current spot.

Read the warning that appears on the screen. Apparently, someone has been accessing the PDA from a remote location, and that access is unauthorized. It also seems that the source of the entry is *off the global grid*. Give a moment's thought to

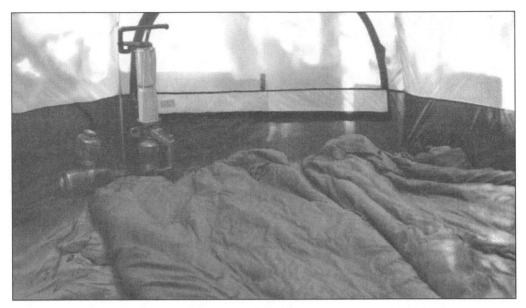

FIGURE 2.2: You soon discover Max and Lilah's tent.

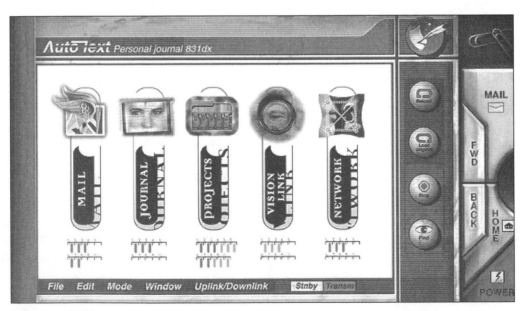

FIGURE 2.3: Pick up the PDA, and then turn it on by clicking its power button.

what that might mean, and then click on Continue to move to the PDA's main menu screen. There are many items that you can look through. Your options are

- Mail
- Journal
- Projects
- Vision Link
- Network

Mail

In the Mailbox, you have the opportunity to learn about Max's and Lilah's life, to find out more about the Ceres Project, and to watch some home movies that they made (see Figure 2.4). All of this information is vital, so study it carefully. The following items are found in the Mailbox's Outbox:

- **Hi guys**—This is a movie that Max and Lilah filmed while camping. They are going to send it back to the staff at Ceres. It shows a human side to this genius couple. It also shows their affection for each other.

- **Obsidian Growth log**—This video shows the growth of the structure over time.

In the Inbox, you can do the following:

- Read the "Awful Day" journal entry. It will provide you with some insight into the Ceres Project. This e-mail was sent by a friend of Lilah's. Within it is an e-mail that Lilah had originally sent to her friend back when Ceres was floundering

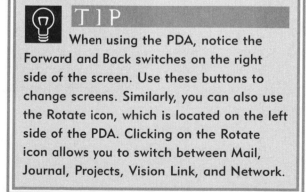

TIP

When using the PDA, notice the Forward and Back switches on the right side of the screen. Use these buttons to change screens. Similarly, you can also use the Rotate icon, which is located on the left side of the PDA. Clicking on the Rotate icon allows you to switch between Mail, Journal, Projects, Vision Link, and Network.

FIGURE 2.4: Viewing movies in the mailbox provides you with insight into Max's and Lilah's background and their current situation.

and emergencies were an everyday occurrence. Things have been much better since then.

◉ Read the "Conference Reminder" journal entry. Lilah is to be a keynote speaker at an upcoming nanotechnology conference in Japan.

◉ View the "Bon Voyage" video that was filmed as Max and Lilah were leaving for vacation. It gives you a feel for the people who have made Ceres a reality.

Journal

In the Journal, you will find three entries:

◉ 5/13/66

◉ 5/14/66

◉ 5/17/66

Nano Goes to Washington

A few years back, one of the luminaries of nanotechnology, Eric Drexler, was summoned to Washington, D.C. to testify before Congress. The following is a brief exchange between him and Vice President Al Gore.

Gore: The way we make things now, we take some substance in bulk and then whittle down the bulk to the size of the component we need, and then put different components together, and make something. What you're describing with the phrase *molecular nanotechnology* is a completely different approach, which rests on the principle that your first building block is the molecule itself. And you're saying that we have all the basic research breakthroughs that we need to build things one molecule at a time—all we need is the applications of the research necessary to really do it?

Drexler: Yes.

Sure, it's not your style to go through others' private diaries, but this is a different situation (see Figure 2.5). These entries provide essential clues to what has happened to Max and Lilah during the last few weeks. It would be a good idea to check them all very carefully.

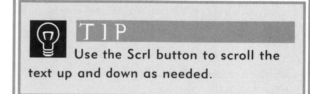

TIP

Use the Scrl button to scroll the text up and down as needed.

Projects

In the Projects section of the PDA, you will find the following files:

- Download speech prep
- Dream—spider
- Nano quotes
- Ceres timeline
- Dream—red tape
- PMA

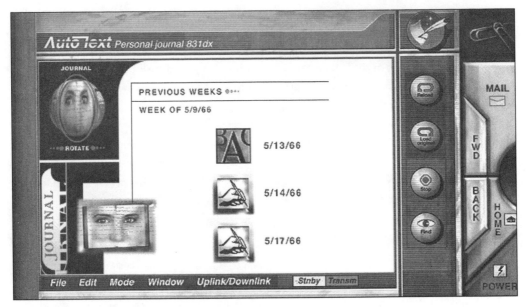

FIGURE 2.5: This is the Journal screen on the PDA.

Under the Folders section of the Project files, you will find the following:

- Ceres
- Viscode Projects
- Papyrus
- Archive
- Personal

Certainly there is a lot to be learned here, as you can see in Figure 2.6. The question is what is really *important*. Sometimes the answer lies in the subconscious. Have you ever had a quite intriguing dream that you forgot the moment you woke up? Well, Max makes a point of keeping a camcorder by his bed to catch those dreams before they're gone.

Max did this, with fear in his eyes, after waking up from a dream about a huge mechanical spider that is at the center of a *machine universe*. He decided the dream was about Ceres. The result is that he put a "crossover switch" into Ceres that would

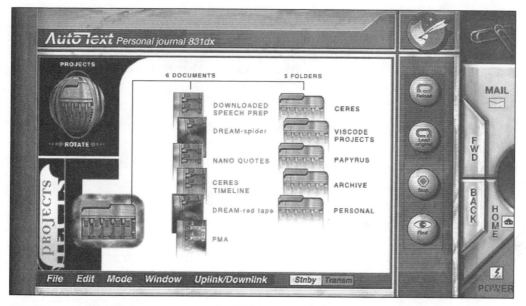

FIGURE 2.6: The Projects screen on the PDA is very enlightening as to the state of Max's and Lilah's subconscious.

allow a human to manually override the computer and shut it down as a last-ditch safety effort.

Lilah's dream is about a confounding bureaucracy in which she literally had to *climb the walls*. The dream made her realize that she would have to defy authority and rebel against the system, if she was ever going to get Ceres through all the red tape that ties up Washington.

The other part that is essential in this section is the Speech Prep. Other elements of the Project section are interesting and can lead to a better understanding of the story, but they are not necessary to progress. Read them and take a good look at the interactive model of the PMA.

LISTEN!

After reading through the items discussed above, leave the tent and turn to your left. Then click forward. You hear a bone-chilling scream. Moving forward, you come upon the base of the Obsidian structure. And isn't that Max's hat on the ground?

Once you're close enough, you can see your reflection in the rock. Does that face look familiar? Have you seen it in one of those movies or journal entries? You have, and it belongs to Lilah! You *are* Lilah!

And so you will be for the rest of this game. But where on earth is Max? Peer into the rock, and, suddenly, you'll find out where he went.

The time has come for you to venture inside *Obsidian*. Chapter 3 takes you into the first world inside *Obsidian*. By mining the PDA for information and then heading toward the glassy face of Obsidian, you've triggered it to suck you inside. Now, your *real* challenge begins.

> **NOTE**
>
> If you try to access either the Vision Link or the Network section of the PDA, you get a message telling you that the Global Network is not currently available. In one of her journal entries, Lilah makes mention of this. She says it almost never happens and wonders if Obsidian could be causing it. Might this be a foreshadowing of events to come?

> **TIP**
>
> The things that you need to access in order to trigger the scream are the three videos on the mail page, the Speech Prep, and the two dream entries.

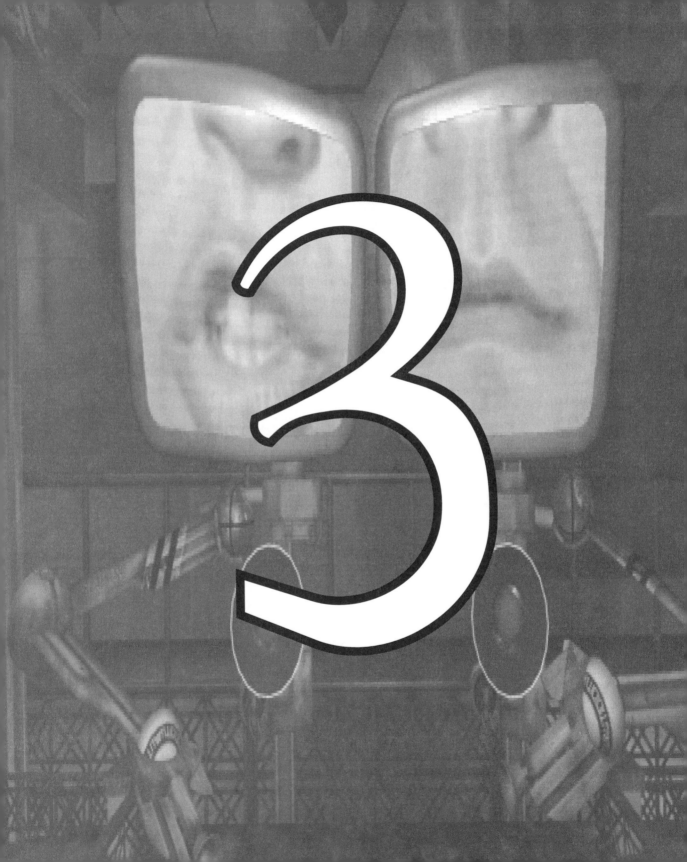

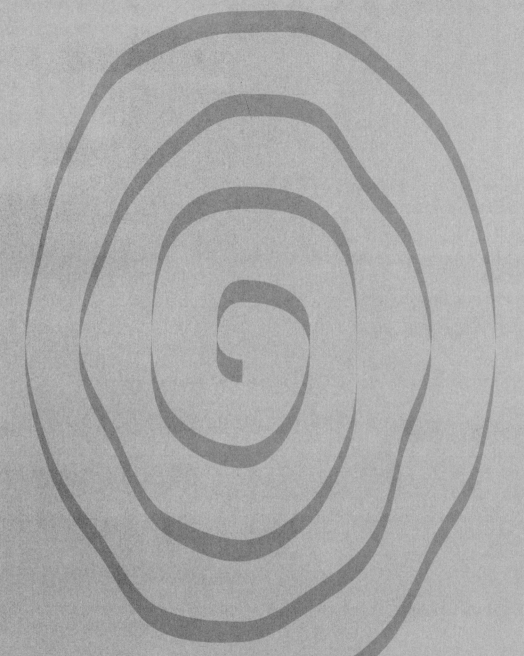

The Bureau Realm

The ominous glass face of the Obsidian structure did more than clear up your true identity. It ushered you into a new world that immediately alters your own sensibilities. You are inside *Obsidian*, where your quest now begins in earnest.

Shrink Rap

Terry Gilliam's film *Brazil*. Kafka's *Penal Colony*. Borges's *Labyrinth*. And of course, above and beyond all else, *Catch 22*. Nightmare visions of control, repression, conformity. Worlds in which the bureaucratic overlords exist to quash your vital life-force, your still, small voice, and to turn you into a drone, a worker bee, or, in this case, a nameless, faceless nanobot.

A booming voice, all power and saccharine, calls to you across a chasm. Here's a bridge for you to cross. Whoops, the bridge is broken. Maybe *you* could fix it. Oh great, a *chore*. And an elevator to lower you into . . .

But wait. He calls you "Lilah!" And now you know for sure—she is who you are. So you think back to the PDA in the forest. Of course, now it's clear why the retinal scan let you in. And that dream you wrote down and sketched, wasn't it about endless red tape? About breaking the rules to get the Ceres Project up and running?

So here you are, in your own dream. Somehow made real, physicalized, for you to relive. Exiting the elevator you run smack into a surly *vidbot*, and just in case you didn't want to commit to this runaround, just in case you didn't want to reach that Bureau Chief, she tells you he's got vital information about Max.

Max, your partner, your genius counterpart, has clearly been taken by the powers-that-be and turned into live bait. Or is he even still alive? You can't know for sure, but if there's a shred of a chance that he is, you've got to get that bridge fixed as soon as possible.

(Continued on next page)

There are signs to help you along your way, but you can't read them. Or can you? In every machine there is a ghost, or a sprite, or perhaps a very tiny mariachi who is way too happy. Here, the mariachi is jamming too hard to remember that old edict about loose lips sinking ships. Stick around and he'll spill it all. Maybe the key word among the rest of these minimum-wage morons is *Obfuscate*, but there's relief behind the guitarrista's red door.

A few of these vidbots mock you blatantly. Others test, or taunt, or play games with you. One of them knows exactly how you can fix the bridge. He names a place for you to go, but of course he doesn't tell you where it is. And the more you explore, the more you realize it isn't here at all.

Maybe you need to do some research, go to the library and hunt around. There are matters in the library of great gravity. Soon you find yourself climbing the walls—literally. The tedium of the first-floor clerks is relieved by the bot-less silence of the Records Face, but now you have a surly computer monitor to deal with.

A filing system should be simple, straightforward, and practical. Unless it's in a dream, in which case it must be lyrical and insane. What's the longest anagram you can make of the words "Filing" and "System"? Where's a good word-mixer when you need one?

By this point, you feel as if everything's upside down. But that's how it should be. And when you're upside down, you can see things in a different way. And if you follow the light, it may take you in different directions.

Perhaps to a maze of cubicles designed to guarantee Bureau security. Are you a security breach? A security risk? Use your eyes and ears. Use them again and again. And while you're at it, let yourself go to the numbingly melodious Muzak. Where would we be without Muzak? In a world, no doubt, too sad and grating to bear.

WADING THROUGH RED TAPE

If there are two words that strike terror in the heart of a true bureaucrat, they have to be "Immediate Action." Think of the DMV and the IRS. Does such a concept even exist within the maddening M.O. of each? So when your travels lead to a booth that bears those two very words, it must be too good to be true.

But that doesn't mean you can't go ahead, as advised, and fix the clocks. Just realize that when things are so backward, as they are here, maybe it's not a full moon but in fact its opposite that merits all the attention.

Just when it seems as if there is no hope, no chance of besting the bureaucrats at their own damn game, an ally appears. Can you trust her? Do you have a choice?

(Continued on next page)

(Continued from previous page)

> Your ally, the Rebel, urges you to make a very important phone call. But the tones you punch out on your touchtone don't create the necessary connection. Don't get bent out of shape. Instead, use your knowledge of shapes and geometrical principles to break through to another dimension.
>
> Between a rock and a hard place—that's where you end up. Only this rock will bow to your will and send you toward your final destination.
>
> The worst bosses, like the Bureau Chief you now encounter, are never overtly cruel, but cruel beyond a fuzzy facade. Can't you just feel the sugary venom? Wouldn't it be great to wreck the Chief's petty fiefdom?
>
> To do that, you need to set the world on its ear. Or, more precisely, the globe. And when you're done, the message is clear: while the bureaucrats may loathe a rebellion, they are no match for your revolutionary fervor.

SUCKED INSIDE THE BUREAU

What is this place? What's going on? Who are these strange creatures? They look like robotic pillbugs that are actually building something with the electricity created by their circuitry.

As you pull back, and back, and back, you realize that these creatures are truly minuscule, perhaps the size of a single cell. That gets you thinking. Are these related to the nanobots you heard about before . . . the ones that do all the work in the Ceres Project?

When completed, this cellular construction has created a building of some kind and an elevator that you are now inside of. A Bureau Chief calls out to you. "Lilah," he says, further confirming your identity from this point on. You recall that *your* dream was about an infuriating bureaucracy, in which you were *climbing the walls*. It seems that, somehow, you are now within a physical re-creation of your own dream (see Figure 3.1). How could this happen? Is it real, or is it imaginary?

The Bureau Chief says that he needs to see you right away, and then he attempts to extend a bridge for you to walk across. The bridge collides with the globe of a giant Atlas statue in the center of the Bureau. The statue makes it impossible for the bridge to reach you. Who *designed* this place, anyway?

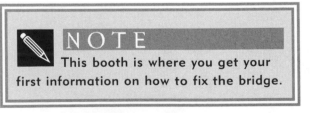

NOTE
This booth is where you get your first information on how to fix the bridge.

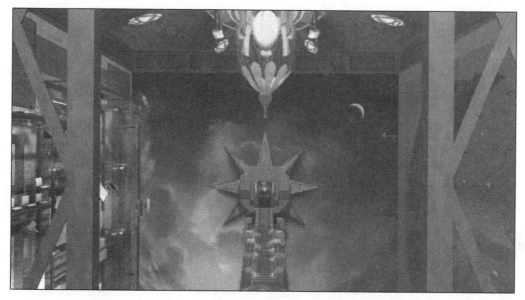

FIGURE 3.1: This is the first view of the Bureau.

The Bureau Chief suggests that you fix the bridge as soon as possible, but at the same time reminds you to go through *proper channels*. Your first tasks, then, are clear: follow the rules and fix the bridge.

As you look around the scene, watch for the cursor to change as you move it on top of elements that you can activate. At the lower portion of your screen is a button to send the elevator down. Press it to travel down to the lower level of the Bureau.

In front of you, there is a desk and a sign (see Figure 3.2). What does the sign say? It is fairly hard to read, but it obviously does says something. There is what looks like a monitor mounted on top of a pole. Read the screen. It says,

> **NOTE**
> Ringing the bell twice after you see the first video clip will get you a different video clip.

> **NOTE**
> The video screens mounted on top of poles are referred to as *vidbots*, which are a cross between robots and video conferencing devices. Whether alive or just programmed, they each seem to have their own personality.

FIGURE 3.2: This looks like a reception desk. What does it say beneath the countertop?

> ### TIP
> Notice the distorted letters that appear beneath the counter of the reception desk. Can you read them? How exactly do you tell what they say? If you click and move to the right of the reception desk, you will face another booth. Click to the right of the booth, and enter a secret room. This is the Glyph Chamber. It will give you specific clues and help on how to decipher all the signs around here.

"Ring Bell." Look for the bell on top of the reception desk. Ring it.

The *vidbot* at the Information booth informs you that the Bureau Chief has information about Max and that you should not keep him waiting. Clearly, you'll have to get that bridge fixed right away.

This main section of the Bureau is divided into ten different vidbot booths. They all have monitors to communicate, while some also include a more specific interface.

VIDBOTS

The vidbots seem to be a dreamy rendering, taken to the extreme, of the standard bureaucrat. There are humans on each of the monitors, each with his or her own personality, but you can never see more than a portion of their faces. The body of each vidbot is completely mechanical. So, are they alive or are they robots? Are they actually present before you, or are they *broadcasting* from somewhere else? None of this is very clear. Nor is it clear how everyone knows who you are, and what you're trying to do.

The Glyph Chamber

When you turn to the right, after finishing with the first vidbot, you see a door off in the distance. Head for it. It leads to the Glyph Chamber. Just as in a dream, where images don't fit together in any rational way, this room seems to bear no resemblance to the rest of the Bureau. It's got some sort of island theme, like a surrealist painting by Salvador Dali. There are even crickets chirping all around you.

The Ultimate Dream Shrink

Carl Jung, who learned from Sigmund Freud and then broke from him, is perhaps the most important figure in contemporary dream analysis. His theories of the psyche, the unconscious, and the "archetype" have continued to resonate long since his death. Consider this passage from his work:

> No amount of skepticism and criticism has yet enabled me to regard dreams as negligible occurrences. Often they appear senseless, but it is obviously we who lack the sense and ingenuity to read the enigmatic message from the nocturnal self. Nobody doubts the importance of conscious experience; why then should we doubt the significance of unconscious happenings?

On the World Wide Web, you can find a treasure trove of information about Jung, his work, and his torchbearers. The best and most complete site is The Carl Jung Anthology at http://www.enteract.com/~jwalz/Jung/

When you click on the book, all of a sudden a miniature mariachi street musician appears. This mariachi seems to be in charge of the book. Every time you click on the book, the page turns. When you're at a blank page, and you click on the mariachi, he strums his guitar to the background music. This strumming causes a letter to appear on the page and rotate in three dimensions about its left axis, as shown in Figure 3.3. This is, in fact, how the signs outside in the main space have been created. Knowing

FIGURE 3.3: See how the letters appear as 3D animations that have been rotated in 3D about their left axis.

this, and going through the extruded alphabet a few times, will make it easy to read all the signs.

Before you leave the Glyph Chamber, make sure to spend time *jamming* with your mariachi pal. It turns out that the piece of music he's playing to is almost five minutes long. Every time he plays, it's a different riff. No matter what chord he plays, though, it's always the right lick at the right time.

When you leave the Glyph Chamber, turn to your right. Turn right again and you're facing the Hints booth.

Booth #1: Hints

At the Hints booth, the vidbot there asks you if you would like some hints. Click *yes*. She will give you various responses, such as "don't cross a bridge until you

come to it," or "the Bureau Chief respects you if you respect yourself." These are not hints at all. They are homilies, designed to make you groan. What you expect are a few pointers about the realm, not some sort of mechanized Emily Post.

Now, turn to the left and then go forward through the swinging door. Turn to your left again, where you'll find a kiosk.

ABOUT THE KIOSK Click on the kiosk button. You hear an automated docent, in ominous tones, describe the history of the bureaucracy. She tells of a horrific rebel-

lion, in which infidels attempted to defy the order and precision of this world. She makes certain to mention that these rebels tried to *reorient*, using any spherical surface, not the officially sanctioned *reorientation ramps*. She mentions that the uprising was quashed, yet pockets of resistance still remain.

These points—about rebels, about sanctioned and unsanctioned reorientation, and about spherical objects—all seem to be important to the unfolding story. But what is *reorientation*, anyway?

Booth #2: Sources

Turn around, and you are facing the Sources. Click on the vidbot and watch what happens. This booth, with a wink and a nod, pays homage to *Myst*, the most successful graphic adventure game of all time. Those blue pages that you heard about endlessly in *Myst* actually play no role here at all. It's just a joke.

Booth #3: Travel

Next you arrive at the Travel booth. The Travel vidbot provides a video tour of all

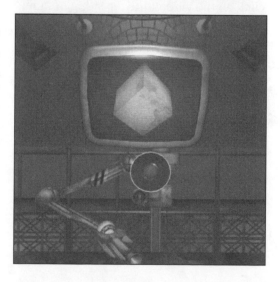

six *faces* in the Bureau. There's the Atlas Face, where you are currently; the Records Face, the Nexus Face, the Security Face, the Time Face, and the Executive Face. So, far, though, these last five faces aren't accessible. Where are they? How do you get there?

Booth #4: Productivity

In a booth with the name Productivity, you'd expect something that gets down to business. Instead, you get a *Breakout* game. Consider it a twisted joke in the construction of this nightmarish office. But while you're here, stop and play awhile. The game is fully operational. While it won't help you fix the bridge, it *will* help you waste a few minutes.

Booth #5: Operations

When you enter the Operations booth and click on the vidbot, the repeating number sequences yield to a strange vision. On the screen appears some sort of hybrid

> ✎ **NOTE**
>
> On your way from the Operations booth to the other side of the Atlas Face, turn and face the Atlas statue. Look up, and get a great angle on him. From the big musical fanfare that accompanies this view, it appears that the statue will eventually be of some great importance.

woman, made seemingly of porcelain with a glowing ring rising out of her head. She turns to address you briefly, mentions your dream, and then disappears. This seems like it's very meaningful, but at present that meaning is far from apparent.

Booth #6: Mediation

It turns out that the vidbots employed to resolve all conflicts can't stop fighting among themselves. Sound familiar? The pair of vidbots shown in Figure 3.4 may remind you of an old married couple who spend a lot of time fighting and bickering.

Booth #7: Bridge Repair

The name of this booth itself makes it seem important. Watch and listen carefully here. The vidbot explains how to get the bridge operational again. If you miss

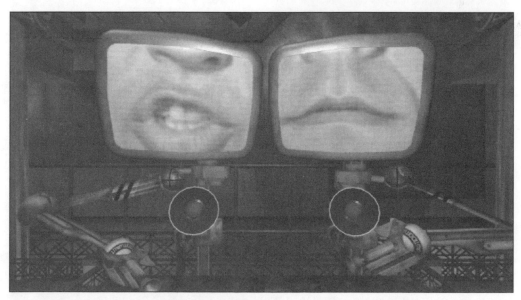

FIGURE 3.4: These two vidbots can't seem to mediate their own conflicts.

the instructions the first time, click on the
vidbot again, and it will print a *carbon copy*.
The instructions are as follows:

"Retrieve a document that is filed under
'Standard Damage,' and then take it to the
department of pre-approvals."

Sounds a little like the DMV, doesn't it?

Booth #8: Reception

If you thought a booth called "Reception"
would welcome you to the Bureau, think
again. It turns out that the name refers to *video*
reception. And for some reason this monitor
receives random snippets of educational
movies from the 1950s. One of these infor-
mative little movies will show you proper eti-
quette and dance steps, in case you missed
them during junior high school.

Booth #9: Bureau of Hygiene

Click on the vidbot at the Bureau of Hygiene,
and he will notice that there is a spot on his
screen. How ironic that the vidbot in charge
of hygiene has a spot. Keep clicking on him,
and he'll get a little frustrated with you.

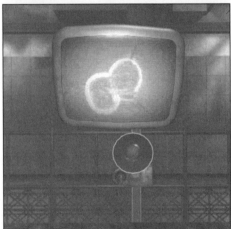

Booth #10: Rebel Control

The Rebel Control booth echoes the themes
of rebellion and repression heard elsewhere
on the Atlas Face. The vidbot exhibits insane
paranoia, as if these rebels are a life-and-
death issue. He asks you if you've seen
rebels "wearing the sign of the sphere." He
wants to know if there are extra Os in your
alphabet soup. Huh?? Like others here, he

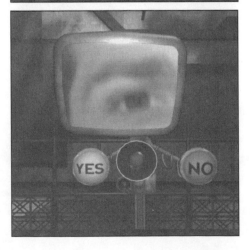

seems to be afraid of any circular or spherical object. Follow as many branches of conversation as you'd like. No matter what branch you take, though, he always ends up in complete hysteria.

THE SUNKEN LIBRARY

When you leave the Rebel Control booth, turn left and move forward. This takes you inside the library, as shown in Figure 3.5. Now turn to your left. You're facing a bookcase. But something's amiss here

> **TIP**
> The document you are now looking for cannot be found in any of the booths. You need to explore another part of the space. Try the library.

because the books are on the floor and the ceiling. Pull out a colored book and let it drop. It falls to the side. This is a clue about what will happen next.

Turn to your right. In front of you is a strange metal slide. Click on it, and it turns out to be one of those sanctioned *reorientation ramps*. What does that mean? Well,

FIGURE 3.5: Something's amiss at the Sunken Library.

when you cross over it, you reorient your gravity to another surface. You are now standing upright on what used to be a wall, as shown in Figure 3.6.

Turn left and proceed toward the ladder on your left. Climb it. Move forward and up the ladder. You'll get a clearer idea of where you are headed now, as the Atlas Face appears across from you. It has gone from being your floor to being your wall.

The ladder takes you up to the elevator again, but now, because you've reoriented, the elevator is lying on its back. Get in and ride it like a mining car, backward, and it will take you across the otherwise impassable library and onto the Records Face. This, you may surmise, is where you can look for that Bridge Repair Document.

THE RECORDS FACE

If this is anything like a filing system in the waking world, then all you have to do now is look under "Standard Damage" for your document. Use the alphabetical signs on the filing rows. Search for Standard . . . no go. Search for Damage . . . same result.

FIGURE 3.6: After your gravity is reoriented, you find yourself standing upright on a wall.

Search randomly for a bunch of documents. It turns out that the documents don't match their filing titles at all. These documents themselves are as bizarre as this whole bureau. Retrace your steps to the elevator; you're going to have to do this another way.

Make sure you're facing the library, and find the CRT screen to your left. There is a message from Max right there on the screen. He's alive, and apparently he's hacked into the circuitry. Before long, though, the terminal cuts him off. As soon as he's gone, you see "Welcome to the Bureau Network" on the monitor. Press Enter *on your keyboard* to display the main menu.

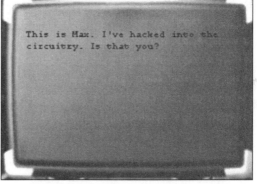

Maybe this CRT terminal can help you find that document. Access it and try. Your options appear on the main menu.

The Main Menu

On the CRT, the main menu presents you with the following numbered list:

1. Find Any Document

2. Search All Databases

3. Telnet to Another Department

4. Play a Game

5. Cloud Ring

You discover options 1 and 2 don't work. So, you try option 3, Telnet to Another Department, to see if that one works.

"Why would you do that?" the terminal asks you. "Don't you like me?"

CLOUD RING Because it appears that the one option out of place on this menu is option 5, Cloud Ring, try it now. Suddenly, the terminal morphs into a portal and you click forward and move into a . . . meadow? (See Figure 3.7.)

You have entered your first *balcony* in *Obsidian*. Here, the word *balcony* refers to a place you reach via an impossible, dreamlike transition. This *is* a dream, remember, and as surreal as dreams can be. So, expect to find a number of these balconies as you progress.

Grab a piece of the cloud and see what happens. Drag it around the screen. If you take it beneath the landscape, it will change into a letter. Try this a couple of times and see what letters appear when you drag all the pieces beneath the surface: a C, an L, an O, a U, and a D. That spells CLOUD. That can't be what you're supposed to spell. Try something else. Grab the pieces of the ring and see what happens. The same thing: an R, an I, an N, and a G appear. RING?

For the solution here, you need a six-letter word. It has to be made from the letters in *cloud* and *ring*. It has to fill up the missing spaces in the . . . GROUND. That's it! As soon as you solve this puzzle, you'll watch a cool animation of a pastoral rain

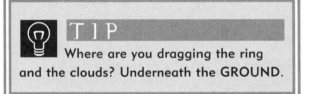
TIP
Where are you dragging the ring and the clouds? Underneath the GROUND.

FIGURE 3.7: This meadow with the clouds and rings is your first balcony.

shower. Turn around and you'll find yourself again at the terminal in the Records Face where you started.

Once you solve the puzzle, menu option 5 changes to this:

"Cloud Ring - > Ground."

Pressing it outputs: "What's the longest word you can make with the letters in [cloud ring]? Ground." This is a hint.

PLAY A GAME Your remaining choices at the terminal are the following:

1. Good Games

2. Dumb Games

3. Word Games

4. Return to Main Menu

Try Good Games. You will find the following choices:

1. Guess the Animal

2. Guess the Number

3. Return to Game Choices Menu

Guess the Animal is a game that only a computer could love. And why? Because it's built using an actual artificial intelligence engine. Each time you play a round in the game, the computer learns from its mistakes, as well as from your input, and gets smarter. If you have the time and the inclination, try to play long enough so that the computer becomes smart enough to win.

Now try the Guess the Animal option. Here is a sample dialogue from this game:

Are you thinking of an animal? Y/N (Answer Y or N for yes or no.)

Yes.

Does it have fur?

No.

Is it an Iguana?

No.

I give up.

Then you can give it a question to distinguish your animal. Enter a question, and the computer will remember it and ask it to you next time you play. Make sure to include a question mark; otherwise, it won't recognize the sentence as a question.

If you select the Guess the Number option, the computer asks you to think of a number. Then it will guess. If it is the wrong number, the computer will call you a liar. If it is the correct one, then the computer will tell you that that game is too easy. It seems as if there's an artificial smart-ass playing here.

DUMB GAMES There are two games under the Dumb Games section. But the computer refuses to play a dumb game. That leaves you with one alternative: Word Games.

For the Word Games option you are given the following three choices:

1. Word Mixer
2. Hangman
3. Return to Main Menu

When you get to this point, give Hangman a quick try and then select Word Mixer. It seems as if this word mixer follows up on the example of the Cloud Ring. When you mix the letters from two words here, you find another longer word—an anagram. Type the words that you want to mix. How about *Standard Damage?* The computer will ask you what you think the longest word is that can be made out of the letters in those two words. Perhaps *Stand* is the correct answer? Wrong. It will give you the answer. The correct answer is TRADESMAN. This is an essential piece of information for completing this realm.

> **NOTE**
> This word mixer, built into the game, is an actual anagram engine. It includes all the words in a concise English dictionary. Before you continue on your merry way, go ahead and play with it. It will mix any words you want. Have fun, go crazy, and amaze your friends.

FIND THE FILING CABINET

Now go look up *tradesman* in the filing cabinet. The filing cabinets are arranged alphabetically. *Tradesman* can be found in the "TOSS–TRAN" drawer, as shown in Figure 3.8. You can move forward and backward in the filing cabinet, using the single arrows for one record at a time, or the double arrows for groups at a time. Keep looking through the drawer until you find the *tradesman* file. When you get to it, open it up and you'll see a document on Bridge Repair. Grab it and go!

HEAD FOR THE NEXUS FACE

Where did that Bridge Repair vidbot say to take this document? In case you forgot, you'll need to head to the Department of Pre-Approvals. But how do you get there from here?

On the opposite side of the Records Face from the library, there is a red slide. Find it and pass over it. It turns out to be another reorientation ramp. Once again, your gravity has shifted. You are now standing on what used to be the ceiling! Go forward to the light, as shown in Figure 3.9. Click on the lever. Drag it left or right. Notice that the light fixture turns around and alters your position in the space.

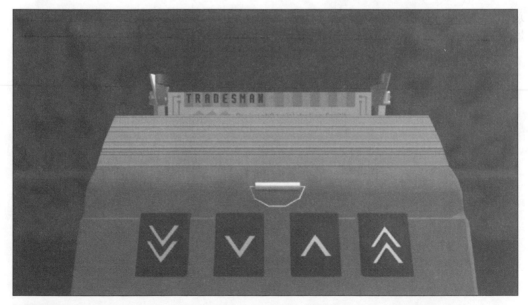

FIGURE 3.8: Use the arrow keys to search the TOSS–TRAN drawer and find *tradesman*.

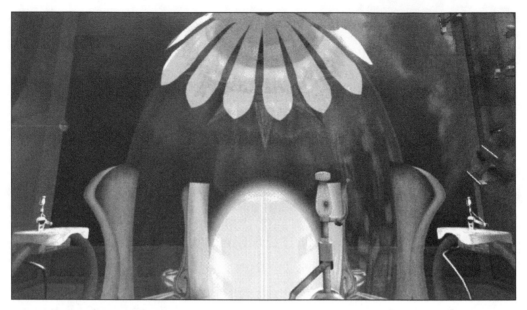

FIGURE 3.9: Go to the light at the center of the Nexus, and click on the lever to the right.

> ## TIP
>
> It may be difficult to figure out if you are moving or if the room is rotating. If you move the lever to the left, you are rotating your position clockwise. Move the lever to the right, and you'll move counterclockwise. The specific solution here is to turn so the wall of cubicles is behind you.

Look around the room and see how you are oriented. Remember the vidbot talking about the passage to the *tempered glass*. Look around and see if you can spot some tempered glass. Click on the lever to move the light fixture so that the maze of cubicles is directly behind you. This maze is called the Security Face. Go back down the slide shown in Figure 3.10 to get to the Department of Pre-Approvals.

DEPARTMENT OF PRE-APPROVALS

See where you are entering the maze? When you get there, you find a friendly little vidbot ready to grant your passage into the maze in return for a favor. She asks you to put in a good word for her with the Bureau Chief. She's in desperate need of a raise. At first she kisses up to you. But each time you keep coming back to get a new set of

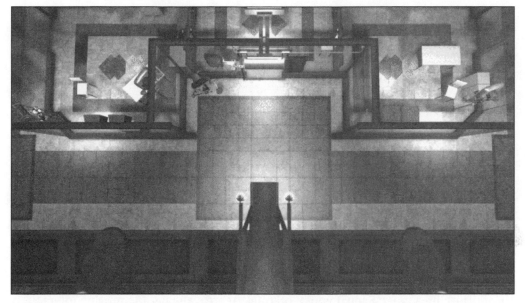

FIGURE 3.10: Go down this slide toward the Department of Pre-Approvals.

cards, she grows more and more surly. It might be fun, before you follow the solution instructions, to watch her demonic progression.

The Cubicles and their functions are as follows:

1. Security Clearance—He takes your picture.

2. Lounge/Reception Area—She tells you to grab a snack.

3. Personality Screening—He shows you ink blots and ask you what you see.

4. Personnel/HR—She shows you pictures of her family.

5. Security Screening (security cameras)—He gives you forms to fill out.

6. Hearing Tests—He tests your hearing.

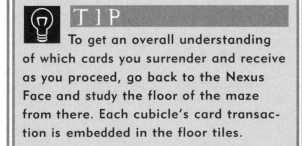

TIP

To get an overall understanding of which cards you surrender and receive as you proceed, go back to the Nexus Face and study the floor of the maze from there. Each cubicle's card transaction is embedded in the floor tiles.

7. Pre-Approvals—She stamps your form and send you on your way.

8. Document Security—He keeps shredding documents.

9. Eye Tests—He tests your vision.

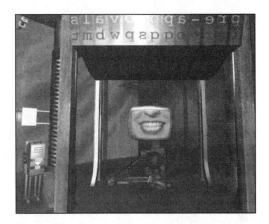

Pay attention to the cards you exchange each time you go into a cubicle. Sometimes you don't have the right cards and can't enter a cubicle. That is the key to this maze. You need to travel from cubicle to cubicle, in the right order—that is, avoiding some and revisiting others—until you have the right cards that admit you to Pre-Approvals.

The good news about the maze is that the vidbots are a blast. Even if you're off track, there's always an amusing interaction to be found. And what about that music, huh? It gets inside your skull, like Muzak.

NOTE

If you enter the cubicle maze without the proper Bridge Repair document, the Pre-Approvals vidbot will tell you to go back and get it.

WARNING

If you exit the cubicle maze at any point by going through one of the side tempered-glass doors, you will lose all the access cards you've gained and have to start over from the beginning of the maze.

The main thing to hunt for in this maze are black cards. Once you're comfortable with the space, think about ways to accumulate black cards. The most helpful vidbots in that quest are the Eye Guy and the Ear Guy.

Also, make sure you don't leave the maze as you're gathering cards. With every exit, you must surrender all your cards and start again.

This can get very confusing and frustrating very easily. Use the following directions to successfully reach the Department of Pre-Approvals, by going to the following cubicles in this order: 3 6 5 8 9 6 9 6 9 6 9 6 9 6 5 2 1 4 1 4 7.

When you make your way to the Department of Pre-Approvals, the vidbot greets you warmly and stamps your document. It goes into your inventory. The vid-bot tells you to rush it over to Immediate Action, and they will get right on it. Hmmm, a bit of a runaround, huh? And yet, it *does* feel as if you're getting closer to fixing that bridge.

There is only one way out of the cubicle maze at this point. It is to your left.

IMMEDIATE ACTION (THE TIME FACE)

To reach Immediate Action, you need to go back to the Nexus. That means you must head back up the red slide and then, using a process of elimination, see which parts of the Bureau you have not visited yet.

Once you have rotated the Nexus, walk back down the red slide toward Immediate Action. You wonder, as you go, why a place that's supposed to help you immediately is filled with chairs and stantions. A Britbot will greets you at the booth. Then, to your consternation, he says he can't help you because the clocks are all broken. It seems that it's up to you to do the fixing (see Figure 3.11).

Go around the vidbot's kiosk and you'll find the clockworks. Sure enough, it has stopped working. The problem, as you can find out by pulling the lever, is that the celestial bodies keep colliding instead of passing by one another.

There are several solutions to this problem. The easiest is as follows:

- Turn the Sun dial four beeps counterclockwise.

- Turn the Moon dial four beeps clockwise.

- Turn the Earth dial two beeps clockwise.

Pull the lever to find out if the solution is in place. If it is not, the clock will run for a short time until the celestial bodies collide. The bottom button on the controls will reset the clock at any time.

If you have fixed the celestial puzzle, return to the Immediate Action booth, and notice how the clocks are spinning wildly. This is not a good sign. Present yourself to the Immediate Action vidbot.

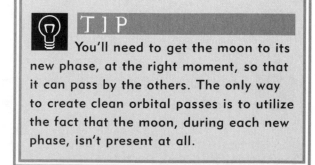

TIP

You'll need to get the moon to its new phase, at the right moment, so that it can pass by the others. The only way to create clean orbital passes is to utilize the fact that the moon, during each new phase, isn't present at all.

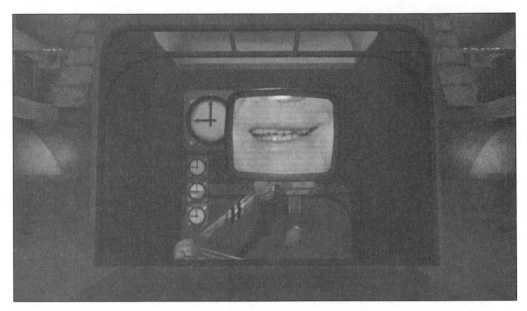

FIGURE 3.11: Immediate Action can't do even a delayed action until you fix the clocks.

He's glad you have the stamped document, and he's thrilled you fixed the clocks, but there's a slight problem—a *backlog*. He'll be ready to process your request . . . in a year. Wait a minute. You went through all that trouble to get the bridge fixed, so that you could reach your friend, Max, and now this?! Just as you're beginning to despair, you hear a whisper coming from nearby. It says, "Meet me at the light."

You may wonder, what does "Meet me at the light" mean? Think back to when you first entered the Bureau. The light was at the top of the room, above the bridge. But now, things are all turned around. However, you were only able to get to the cubicle maze by going right by the light. The light is at the center of the Nexus Face. It's on the platform that allows you to revolve to the different orientation ramps.

Leave the Immediate Action kiosk and head back to the light. When you get

> **TIP**
> Flip the lever on the right, and make sure that the Nexus turns counterclockwise like a light bulb.

> **NOTE**
> If it appears that the room is moving, and not the Nexus, don't be fooled. Really, the only thing that is moving is the Nexus.

there, the voice tells you to turn off the lights. How do you do that? Well, you know you can turn the platform around and around, and that's the same way you unscrew a light bulb, as you see in Figure 3.12. So, keep turning around on the platform, counterclockwise, by pulling that lever over and over, and see what happens. After a number of revolutions, the lights go out and you meet the *Rebel*.

When the lights are all the way out, the Rebel welcomes you to her rebellion. She says the bureaucracy will never help you. Sticking with her is the only way to get to Max. She says that there's another way to get around the space and that it can be found in a document filed under the words "Orient Militia."

The End of Logic?

In the beginning of this century, artists and philosophers began to have great doubts about the preeminence of the rational mind. The world was in a state of destructive chaos. Human beings, with all their advances, seemed determined to destroy themselves.

At the same time, Sigmund Freud, with his theories of the unconscious and of free-association, was positing a creative force that existed just beyond rational thought. The question became: how do we get there?

One answer to this question was surrealism. *Surrealism* refers to words, images, and actions that make no seeming sense and yet seem to strike a chord deep within us. In this way, they manage to bypass the rational mind and take us straight into our psychic depths.

André Breton, an early surrealist pioneer, described the approach this way, in his essay "What Is Surrealism?"

> *Surrealism rests in the belief in the superior reality of certain forms of association neglected heretofore; in the omnipotence of the dream and in the disinterested play of thought.*

This all may sound very heavy, but it leads to art that is as hysterical as it is profound. If you're laughing at some part of *Obsidian*, and you don't know why it's funny—that's surrealism!

Breton's entire essay, along with tons of information about surrealism and its sister movement, dadaism, can be found at the Web site !Surrealisme! at the following address:
http://pharmdec.wustl.edu/juju/surr/surrealism.html

This site includes a wonderfully absurd device called a "Surrealist Compliment Generator." Why not pull up a few compliments, and then lay them on your unsuspecting friends?

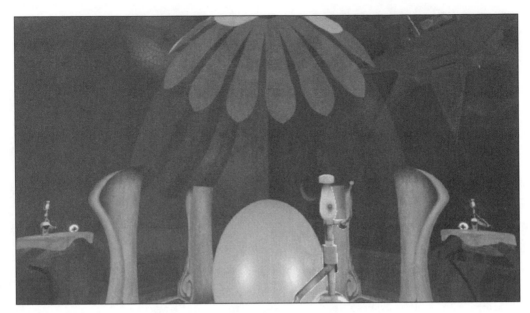

FIGURE 3.12: Turn the Nexus to unscrew it like a light bulb.

This happened once before, when you were looking for a file under Standard Damage. You now understand that you must learn the longest anagram that can be made my mixing the words *Orient* and *Militia,* and then the correct file will be located under that word. You could sit down and figure it out, but there's an easier way. Go to the Records Face, visit the CRT terminal, and get Word Mixer to give you the answer. The answer is *Limitation.* This document can be found in the drawer labeled Leso–Ling.

The Limitation document shown in Figure 3.13 shows a diagram of a cube. Could this be the cube that you are in currently? And what is the purpose of the Limitation document? It seems to be showing coordinates within the cube. You will also notice that the number 934 appears on the document. But how does this help?

Leave the Filing Room and go back to the Nexus. Turn yourself so that the Executive Face, with the sky mural, is behind you. Then turn around and go toward it. There's something in front of the mural that looks like another puzzle. Play with it awhile. Hit the button on the right. It seems to be a strange kind of phone.

The Phone Puzzle

When you're ready to get serious here, place the code 934 in the top-right corner. Suddenly, a cube representing the Bureau appears and unfolds itself onto the phone's

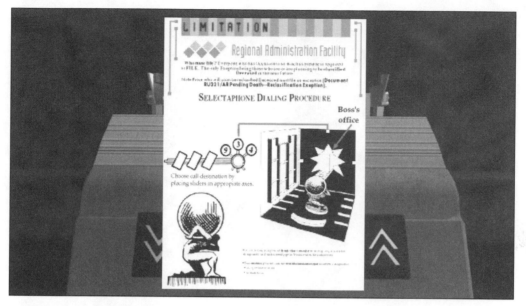

FIGURE 3.13: The Limitation Document shows a diagram of a cube.

grid. The red lines across the unfolded cube can slide up and down. Where you slide them determines which part of the Bureau you call. Now that you have more information, play around a little while longer. Who do you need to call most? The Bureau Chief, of course. He's the one with information about Max.

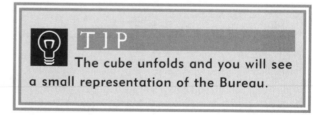

TIP

The cube unfolds and you will see a small representation of the Bureau.

It seems that you call whoever is located at the intersection of the lines. As shown in Figure 3.14, the faces of the Bureau are laid out from left to right as follows:

- First Square: The Records Face is on top, and the Atlas Face (where the vidbots are) is on the bottom.

- Second Square: The Nexus Face (ceiling) is on top, and the Security Face is on the bottom.

- Third Square: The Time Face is on top, and the Executive Face is on the bottom.

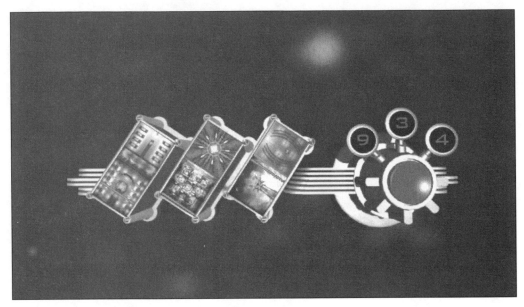

FIGURE 3.14: This is how the Bureau's faces are laid out.

The three lines across the unfolded sides of the cube represent planes that spread across the three-dimensional space. If you remember your high school geometry, they represent the x, y, and z axes; that is, horizontal, vertical, and depth. When two of these planes intersect, their intersection creates a line. When three of them intersect, their intersection defines a single point.

Whenever these three lines are placed so that they intersect inside the cube, you will be designating a unique point in the space. If you hit the dialing button, you can call that point. If someone's there, you'll get an answer.

The line on the left needs to be placed against the wall where the Bureau Chief sits. If you remember, he's on the

> **TIP**
>
> Think of the sliders as three-dimensional planes extending out from each wall. Now search for an intersection of those three planes that will designate the Bureau Chief's office.

> **NOTE**
>
> If the lines aren't placed so that they intersect, you'll get a message about dialing incorrectly.

opposite end of the Atlas Face from the sunken library. So place that line flush against the bottom.

The line in the center needs to be placed at exactly the height of the Chief's office, which turns out to be directly in the middle of the cubicle maze. So place this line in the maze's center. By this point, you have chosen an intersection of planes that are the correct height, and on the correct wall, but what remains is to specify exactly what point along that line you want to designate.

The third setting, then, is the easiest. Place it right through the depiction of the Chief's office. You've succeeded (see Figure 3.15). Now call the Chief. Notice the suspicion aroused by your call, but be glad he's letting you through to a secret form of orientation. Why? Because, you can surmise, there is no public form of reorientation that can get you to the Chief. After a short, one-sided conversation, you are allowed to pass.

Balancing Rock Balcony

This puzzle takes place on a gorgeous stretch of beach, with torches blazing and with gravity, once again, acting very strangely. Play with the big triangular rock. Notice

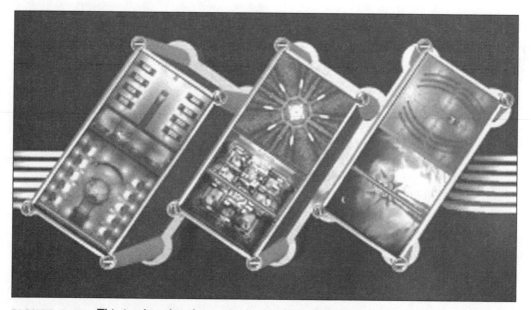

FIGURE 3.15: This is what the phone puzzle should look like before you place the call. Note the positions of the lines on each face.

how the rock balancing on it is not affected. By now, you've come to expect impossible, dreamlike moments like this.

You can balance and move the big rock in five directions: up, left, right, backward, and forward.

OK, so move the rock around. What seems to happen? It's hard to tell until you exit the balcony and reenter the Bureau. Hey, wait a minute! If you've left the rock in a different position, the Bureau will be in a different position as well. Where you reenter the Bureau, from this balcony, is always determined by how you've left the rock.

The Solution: pull the rock, by clicking on the highest spot at its top and dragging it so that it slides in the lowest possible position, directly toward you (see Figure 3.16).

Turn around and go forward to enter the Bureau. You are standing on what is the sky mural of the Executive Face. This is the one place you could not go, using standard reorientation.

Move forward again. At this point, your choices are left or right. If you click right, you will walk around the edge of the mural face and follow a path all the way around what looks like another vidbot sitting in an orange office. It's the Bureau Chief, which is great, and yet something's not right. You can tell immediately.

To greet you, the Chief has to tilt his head all the way back. He tells you that you're standing on his sky and that you need to get your feet on the ground. What he means is that you are in the wrong orientation. Your feet are using the wall behind the Chief's desk as a floor. You need to stand and face him, in the same orientation. But how can you do that, if the only way into his office is across the broken bridge? There's not much left in this realm, obviously, but what do you do now?

From the Bureau Chief's office, turn around and go back one click. Turn left and go to the corner. Turn left again and go forward two clicks. You will find a lattice that serves as a railing down on the Atlas Face. The only thing is, it is turned 90 degrees from how you first saw it. Maybe you'll be able to climb it like a ladder. Try it.

Move in closer by using the right diagonal arrow. Turn left and look up the lattice. Once you do that, start the climb. When you reach the top, you will see a vidbot on one side and be able to move forward. But wait, after moving forward, you can't go

FIGURE 3.16: Pull this floating rock toward you.

any further. A metal gate, one that was used on the Atlas Face to separate the area in front of the Information desk from the rest of the vidbots, opens when you try to walk across it. You seem to be stuck with no way out, except for the possibility of backtracking. You'll have to find another way. Go ahead and climb down from this lattice. Is there another one?

> **T I P**
>
> You have exhausted all standard and elite methods of reorientation, yet you have not been able to meet the Chief with "your feet on the ground." Search for other, perhaps unintentional, methods of reorienting.

There *is* another one, and you have to move a little further around the Executive Face to get to it. You can see it directly across from you as you climb down the lattice that didn't go anywhere. So, try that. After all, the two lattices are parallel to each other.

Click forward twice, and then turn right. Move in closer using the left diagonal arrow. Position yourself directly in front of this lattice by turning right. Now begin your ascent.

Once you are at the top, you'll have a testy encounter with that surly Information vidbot. It will be a fine revenge when you must step on her face to make your way forward. But forward to where? You probably realize by now that the coup de grâce here, the finale of the realm, is to use the Atlas statue itself as a reorientation device.

You might recall that there was a hint to this possibility when you listened to the automated voice at the Atlas kiosk.

Climbing over the Atlas statue takes you right to the bridge. You can walk across it to the master of bureaucracy himself, the Bureau Chief. (See Figure 3.17.)

When you finally get to the Bureau Chief, he rants and raves that you have broken every rule in the book to get to him, but he has orders from higher-ups to pass on some vital information about

> **NOTE**
> Notice that when you step forward and onto the vidbot at the Information booth, the vidbot complains. Isn't it a little fun to torment one of these vidbots—after all, they've been doing that to you for hours?

Max. You wonder: is Max here? Can you talk to him? But, alas, all the Bureau Chief does is pull down a screen and show you a movie.

The movie turns out to be a tour through Max's brain. How this is possible is still unclear. But following along the trail of gray matter and synapses, you see key moments

FIGURE 3.17: The Bureau Chief and his glasses.

in Max's life. There's young Max, reciting a bit from a famous poem by Samuel Taylor Coleridge entitled *Kubla Khan:*

Weave a circle round him thrice,

And close your eyes with holy dread,

For he on honey-dew hath fed,

And drunk the milk of Paradise.

Paradise? Did young Max have a presentiment of the contribution that he would later make to the earth's restoration?

There's also a moment very early in Max's relationship with Lilah. Later, you witness an encounter with Max's and Lilah's boss, in real life, who looks alarmingly like the Bureau Chief you just met in your dream. Finally, there is a memory of Max's awful spider dream. As the memory comes to an end, it seems to expand and fill your view.

Effortlessly, you travel from one dream to the next. One click more, and you find yourself in the Spider realm.

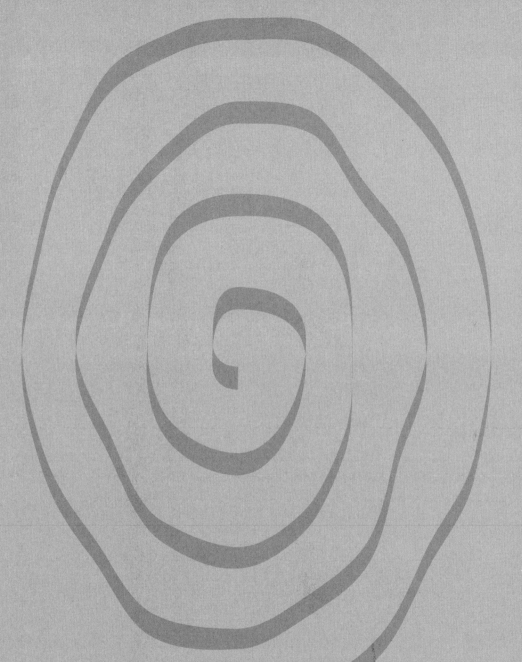

The Spider Realm

After completing the Bureau realm and escaping from its mindless organization, you enter a world that is completely overpowering. The atmosphere seems hot and humid, and all around you are sounds of clanking machines and molten metal. Welcome to the Spider realm.

Shrink Rap

At the farthest reaches of advanced physics, there is an amazing supposition. Stated pure and simple, the supposition goes like this: the universe is a hologram.

What does this mean? The most striking aspect of a hologrammatic image is that no matter how many times you split it, down to the most infinitesimal speck, each part of the hologram contains the entire whole. Taken as a model of the cosmos, this means that every speck of dust contains the whole of creation—past, present, and future. Everything that has ever *been* contains everything that will ever *be*. Everything that has ever existed contains everything else that has ever existed, or will ever exist.

To ponder this is to enter a realm of the mind that scrapes at and challenges all we think we know and understand. It makes no sense at all, but the power of it is completely beyond sense. The great mystics of the world have always warned against the limits of rational thought. They have advocated complete and unconditional surrender of all we think and believe. They call us, in the words of David Byrne, to "stop making sense."

We can't quite figure out how to do this, but luckily we don't have to. Why? Because our dreams do it all for us. Max Powers had a dream of a giant mechanical spider. It posited a parallel universe in which the very life force is mechanical. "In the beginning was the machine." To surrender to his dream is to stop making sense and to let any and all meaning

(Continued on next page)

surface through intuition and association. Where do you go? What do you do? Instead of creating your journey, or mapping out a path, why not let the path come to you?

Another aspect of the spacey realm where the physicist meets the mystic is the following credo: "As without, so within." All you ever search for in the world around you is already present inside of you. All you ever want to achieve or experience is already part of your current totality. The world outside is a reflection of the world within.

If your significant other happens to be too stubborn, and it irks the hell out of you, an expanded perspective challenges you to find the stubbornness within. If your boss's inconsistency is driving you crazy, search for your *own* inconsistency.

So what does this have to with a mechanical spider in a rusty old factory? Outside the spider are a number of devices. Thus, according to this line of reasoning, doesn't it follow that these devices would also exist, in some form, inside the spider? And, if so, why not birth the path and the spider at the very same time?

Ancient alchemy posited four elements at the core of everything. These elements were earth, air, fire, and water. In a machine universe, would the essential elements differ? What would be the building blocks of machine consciousness? To answer this is to find the world in a dream, a universe in a spider, and the seed of a brand-new consciousness. Only by birthing and entering this consciousness can you begin to understand it. Once you understand it, more mundane questions give themselves up freely. Questions such as "Where is Max?" Or "Who is making all these dreams?" And, most important, "Can I finish this damn realm before the sun comes up?"

MASS PRODUCTION

The Spider realm is a large factory, with a giant lifeless mechanical spider perched on a circular platform in its center (see Figure 4.1). You learn that you can travel around the spider and out to the edges of the factory, where there are manufacturing devices you can interact with. These devices each pertain to an essential element of the realm—fire, air, metal, and oil—and to the realm's overall theme.

FIGURE 4.1: The spiderlike structure overlooks the factory floor.

More importantly, though, you also learn that you can climb the rickety scaffolding and enter the spider itself. The portals on the body of the spider lead to *balconies*. Remember the balcony concept; they are dreamlike transitions that lead to places to which one could never physically travel. It is inside these four balconies that the majority of your game play will take place.

But be prepared for two important things before you begin. First, the more you understand the theme of the realm, as evidenced in the factory, the better you will be able to perform your task inside the balconies. Second, notice that there is an oil tower featured prominently in the factory. It seems inaccessible, serving no purpose, but nothing is ever without purpose in these dreamworlds—and the oil tower is no exception.

Also, muse a moment on what the purpose of this factory might be and how the spider might be involved in that purpose. Notice that the factory and the spider itself are rusty and, for the most part, nonfunctioning. Imagine what the factory would be like in full operation, humming with productivity and the manufacturing of . . . what?

In the back of your mind, as all of this triggers associations with what has come before, a realization develops. While the Bureau was your dream of an infuriating bureaucracy, this realm must be Max's dream of . . . the spider, of course. That dream ended horribly, if you recall. It convinced Max to build a hardwired crossover switch into the Ceres Project, one that could easily take the system from machine control to human control. Will your own journey through Max's dream end with equal horror?

A BRIEF REUNION WITH MAX

Your actual starting point in this realm is right along one of the spider's legs. Click toward the leg and find yourself in front of a large grate. Look into the grate and you

will see Max! He seems to be in an entirely different realm, one that is dark, with giant jolts of electricity whizzing by. He looks up and tells you to open that grate and join him right away.

But that's not the only thing he tells you. Thinking things through, he reaches an incredible supposition, one that makes the whole Obsidian structure take on a new dimension.

Max wonders if, in fact, the Obsidian structure is the Ceres Project itself. Could it have become conscious, he asks; ejected its core; and crashed back to earth to seek out its creators?

If Max is right, then you are currently standing inside a giant black mountain that has been built using nanotechnology on the very earth itself, by a *conscious machine!*

The only way to open the grate is to operate a nearby winch. Give it a try. You quickly find that it can only open a little bit, before being stopped by one of the spider's giant mechanical legs. There must be some way to get that grate open, but how? Could you actually find a way to move the spider?

On the backside of the spider is a stairway that travels down to another level, toward a large furnace. Go down the stairway and approach the furnace.

On your way to the furnace, you will find an elevator-like device to your left. Click inside it, and play with the controls. This is a special treat. You find yourself rising through the air, in a cable car that gives you a bird's-eye view of this whole factory.

At the top of the factory, the cable car stops and you can get out. There is a panel with levers before you. Right now, if you pull them, nothing happens. But feel free to come back here again, after you've solved a few puzzles. There may be a few bonuses for you here.

Take the cable car back down to the factory floor. Exit and proceed to the furnace. When you arrive, you will find a lever. Pull the lever and watch the roaring flames fill the firepit. This furnace doesn't do anything else, so why is it here? Is it just a toy, or does the theme of fire play a part in the spider's universe? After you have finished, return to the upper level where the spider stands.

THE FIRE BALCONY

Position yourself on the right side of the spider. You will see a large scaffolding next to one of its tremendous legs. Approach the scaffolding and look up. You will see that the scaffolding looks much like a ladder and is an easy way for you to explore the heights where the balconies are perched. Climb up the scaffolding and you will discover a door. The door is a yellowish orange color and will allow you to enter (see Figure 4.2).

Inside the door you see a small hillside with a moving tree that has five *arms*, or moving branches. The branches sway up and down and touch five glowing posts

> **NOTE**
> There are four scaffoldings around the spider's huge structure. Each scaffolding leads you to a new balcony within the Spider. You may start with any one that you want, but for the sake of the strategy outlined here, start with the Fire balcony. Then tackle the Air balcony, the Metal balcony, and finally the Oil balcony.

FIGURE 4.2: Go through the yellowish orange door to the Fire balcony.

that are in the ground. You also see a hole in the clouds that is not consistent with the background. Reach up and touch the hole in the clouds. Wham! Lightning. The lightning strikes the glowing posts and the tree continues unaffected.

Next, reach up and touch one of the glowing posts. The tree branch that touches that post stops. As you release your mouse button, the tree branch resumes its swaying. Hmmm.

To solve this puzzle, you have two items to work with: the tree branches and the lightning. The key to solving this puzzle lies in timing the branches to touch the posts at the same times as the lightning strikes. Does this sound hard? Well, it is, but you *do* have some important items to help you solve this puzzle. If the lightning and a branch aren't synchronized, you hear nothing special when the lightning strikes a post. But when the lightning strikes a glowing post at the same exact time as the tree branch, it creates a musical note. When more than one branch in a row is correct, the notes combine in a harmonic progression.

When you touch the hole in the clouds, the lightning strikes the post at the furthest right and then continues clockwise, as shown in Figure 4.3. To solve this puzzle, you must adjust the tree branches to follow this order so that the lightning strikes each of the branches as the branches touch the posts. An easier way to complete this is to first get the

TIP

If when you have climbed the scaffolding you encounter a door that is not yellowish orange, you are at the wrong door and should climb down and find the yellowish orange door at the top of one of the other four scaffoldings.

TIP

It is important to listen to the sound played when the lightning strikes the posts.

WARNING

There is no easy solution to this puzzle. It involves sound, timing, and hand-to-eye coordination. It might take a while, but solving it is truly gratifying.

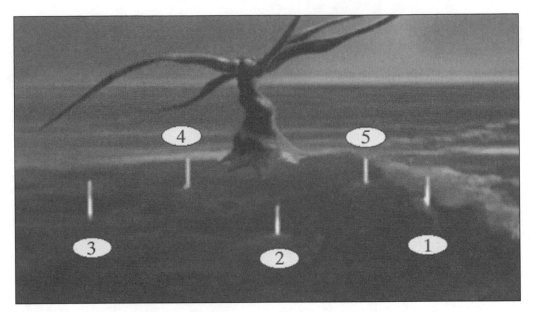

FIGURE 4.3: The lightning strikes the tree with the five posts in this order.

branches in order and then have the lightning strike and listen for the musical notes. If a note sounds on a specific post when the lightning strikes, you have it. Adjust the other branches until they, too, cause a note to sound. If the branches are correct, and you don't hear a note, you have started the lightning just a little out of sync. Keep the branches the same, and adjust your timing with the lightning. After a few tries, that lightning bolt will begin to bend to your will.

When you successfully strike chords on all the posts, the branches wilt to the ground and the tree catches on fire. Congratulations, you've won! This is a small, but truly challenging, puzzle. There is no other puzzle quite like it in *Obsidian*. Have you seen one like it anywhere else?

Now that the tree is flaming, there is nothing more to do here. Turn around and exit.

The Cosmology Room

When you exit the Fire balcony, you expect to travel back to the factory. Instead, you find yourself whirring through space. This is another one of the game's mysterious, magical transitions. You end up in something that looks like a planetarium. It's called the Cosmology room. Soon you will see why.

As you move into the Cosmology room, you find yourself facing a starfield. Then, Max's face seems to appear in a maelstrom of stars, as you can see in Figure 4.4. He's hacked into the intelligence of *Obsidian* again and is communicating with you. Max puts another piece of this puzzling story together.

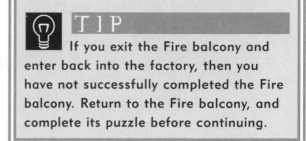

TIP

If you exit the Fire balcony and enter back into the factory, then you have not successfully completed the Fire balcony. Return to the Fire balcony, and complete its puzzle before continuing.

He tells you that this, of course, is *his* dream. He realizes that Ceres must have broken into his journals and yours as well and learned about the dreams there. This makes sense, as you recall that *your* journal was broken into back in the Forest realm. This happened just before you got there, and according to the warning message, a similar break-in occurred around the time Ceres must have become conscious in space.

Max wonders about the obvious questions. Why would a conscious machine be interested in dreams? And why, particularly, would it go ahead and *build* them? Leaving you to think about that, Max disappears again.

In the middle of the starfield you find a floating picture. It's a picture that ought to remind you of the Fire balcony, where you've just been.

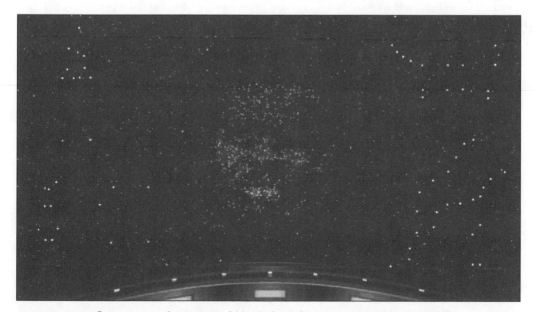

FIGURE 4.4: Can you see the image of Max's face that appears in this starfield?

FIGURE 4.5: This is the starfield control panel. Does the center image remind you of anything?

Move the cursor to the bottom of the screen and scroll down to see the starfield control panel shown in Figure 4.5. Look at the five images on the control panel and see what they represent. Also, notice the image in the center of the control panel. What does it remind you of?

Notice that on the front edge of the control panel there are four slots, each one corresponding to the image above it. Drag your fire image to the slot that corresponds to the fire icon on the control panel and let it go. It should slide right in.

Then, another slew of stars whirs into a maelstrom. The stars go through a morphing process, and then take their place in the night sky as a torch constellation that matches the torch on the starfield control panel. At the same time, you hear the voice of . . . is it a *god* of this universe? The voice intones a kind of biblical poetry.

"In the beginning was the machine," the recitation begins. Then it goes on to mark the difference between "Max" and "us." Who is this "us," you wonder? You're reminded of what Max said about this dream in the PDA: "Instead of fixing the spider itself, I had to fix the universe surrounding it."

It seems that the *machine* being referred to here by the magisterial voice is the spider. And it also seems as if the spider is the progenitor—the Zeus, if you will, of its

How Do You Know You're Conscious?

One of the top thinkers about thought is Marvin Minsky. His work explores consciousness in humans, as well as possible consciousness in machines. This subject is so difficult and abstract that most of us would rather forget about it. But Minsky asks the kind of questions that stick with you. For instance:

How do you know how to move your arm?

How do you locate your memories?

What does meaning mean?

Minsky likes to tweak our assumptions about consciousness. Like this:

I have found that many people maintain that even if a machine were programmed to behave in a manner indistinguishable from a person, it could still not have any subjective experience. Now isn't that a strange belief—considering that unless you were a machine yourself, how could you possibly know such a thing?

More Minsky:

. . . Much of what is commonly attributed to consciousness is mythical. . . . It is one thing to have access to data, but another thing to know how to make good use of it. Knowing how your pancreas works does not make you better at digesting your food. In short, we are not much aware of what our bodies do. We're even less aware of what goes on inside our brains.

own universe. So the "us," just maybe, are the machines that have spawned and evolved in this place.

Now, it makes sense that this is called the Cosmology room. By solving the balcony puzzles that refer to the machine universe's basic elements, you are also learning about the universe's earliest beginnings.

Before you proceed with the rest of the realm, review where you are. You are inside the giant Obsidian structure,

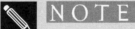 NOTE
If some of this is seeming really *out there* or *trippy*, it is. It's a dream, after all, and it makes strange but bizarre sense in the way many of your own dreams do.

which has been made by the Ceres Project, created by you and Max, and which has come to life in space and chosen to crash back to earth. You know that Ceres has learned about your own and Max's dreams and then gone ahead and used its nanotech powers to build the dreams as real, physical spaces.

Why? At this point you have no idea, but it's easy to imagine that the answer is just around the corner.

When you have completed the torch constellation, turn around and go down the elevator. On the way down, notice how, just for a moment, the mouth of the spider flickers with flame. It turns out that by restoring fire to the universe, you have also brought fire to the spider at the universe's center. It's all, as you've noted, just like Max's dream.

After exiting the elevator, turn around and get your bearings. It turns out that the elevator has brought you down from the oil tower onto the factory floor. The Cosmology room, then, is in that oil tower. Perhaps you'd like to go back up, but that seems to be impossible because the elevator has returned to the top without you. This will always be the case. The only way to get back to that room is by solving another balcony puzzle and making the magical transition. It's maddening that the room is so close, and yet inaccessible by physical transport, but that's the way it is.

THE AIR BALCONY

While circling the spider, approach it from the left, front portion. There will be a scaffolding (the same as in the Fire puzzle). Climb the scaffolding and look around while atop it. You will see an impressive scene of the factory floor. The door at the top of the scaffolding is a light blue color. It is shown in Figure 4.6. Enter it.

After you enter the door, you see a new strange world. In front of you is a mounted gun, and off in the distance is a swirling tornado traveling across the screen, as shown in Figure 4.7. The ground is covered with balls. Grab the gun and shoot a couple of balls. When the balls you shoot hit the ground, a column rises toward the cloud covering.

After you finish exploring this view, look down. You find a pipe where the balls travel upward into the gun, and you

> **NOTE**
>
> If the door's color is not light blue, climb up one of the other scaffoldings until you find the light blue door. Again, you can choose to start at any one door you wish, but for the strategy being laid out here, you will be exploring them in a specific order.

FIGURE 4.6: The door to the Air balcony is light blue.

FIGURE 4.7: After entering through the Air balcony door, you will see a mounted gun and a tornado in the distance.

> **TIP**
> The goal of this realm is to capture the twister by trapping it into a shape and giving the spider his breath of life.

see a cutaway section of pipe with a large ball. Enter the ball.

Once inside, you see a covered box. Go into the box and uncover its contents. You discover a board with the same balls as in the landscape, as shown in Figure 4.8. Part of the board is a dark green and the middle portion is a lighter green. Along the rim of the board, you will see miniature bel-

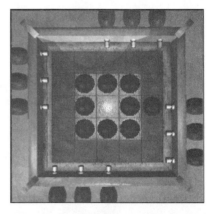

lows. Click on a couple of the miniature bellows and watch the movement of the balls.

Put a couple of the balls into the middle portion of the light green board, and return to the top level with the gun. Shoot a couple of balls and see what happens. Try to shoot them at the twister and see the effect. Then, return back to the bottom level to look at the board again.

When you are back at the board, you realize that the shape made by the shot balls in the landscape above corresponds to the pattern you placed

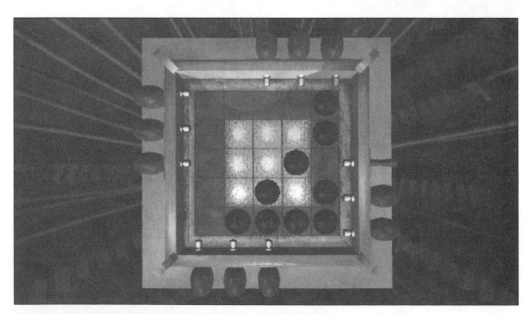

FIGURE 4.8: Inside the ball you will see this board with some more balls.

the balls in down here. So, to capture the twister, you need to make a shape that can succeed in capturing the tornado. This shape, it turns out, is a square with a hollow middle.

Here's a way to make the correct square. First, use the bellows to consolidate the balls into the middle area. Use the leftover ball to keep certain balls in place. The combination of the bellows and the leftover ball will allow you to complete the desired hollow square shape.

Once this has been accomplished, return to the upper level with the gun. Shoot the gun and attempt to surround the twister. This may take a couple of tries because the twister moves around randomly, but sooner or later, you are bound to capture it.

When you make the lucky shot, the twister tries and tries to escape, but to no avail. The twister rattles around, indicating that it has been successfully trapped, and then it slows down and is sucked into the tower cluster. Then the whole landscape appears to be breathing.

Exit the level from the top level, and you will find yourself in the Cosmology room, once again.

> **TIP**
> Cycle the balls around and continue until you make a square with a hollow middle. Use balls to impede the movement of the other balls.

> **WARNING**
> If you exit out to the spider, then you have not successfully completed the puzzle. Return immediately and finish before continuing.

The Cosmology Room Again

Once again, you are in front of the starfield. You also have a new image, this one from the Air balcony, that can be moved down to the lower control panel. Just as you did the first time, insert the picture into the corresponding slot. Once you have done this, look up to learn a new piece of the machine cosmology and to find a new constellation outlined among the stars.

The new constellation is a windsock, representing, of course, the air element that you have just harnessed. There also appear to be some new stars in the center of the field. You can click on them and try to make your own constellation by connecting nearby stars, as you see in Figure 4.9. So far, though, you don't have enough stars to make anything.

Once you have finished this, exit the level through the elevator and return to the factory. On your way down the elevator, notice that the spider seems to sway momentarily from side to side. The breath of life is in it now, thanks to your trapping of the tornado. It seems, in fact, that you are bringing the spider to life! Once it is alive, let's hope it will move off the grate and allow you to get down to Max.

THE METAL BALCONY

Looking at the spider once again, move on to discover the third puzzle of the realm as well as the third element—metal. Your goal now is to set a nonworking factory into motion.

To seek the entrance into the Metal balcony, begin by facing the spider's face. Go around to the left and turn to face the side of the spider. Go to the scaffolding that is on your left. Climb it and enter the shiny silver door shown in Figure 4.10.

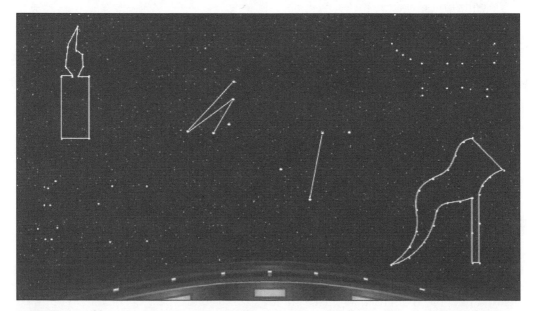

FIGURE 4.9: You can connect stars to make your own constellation, but you will need more stars.

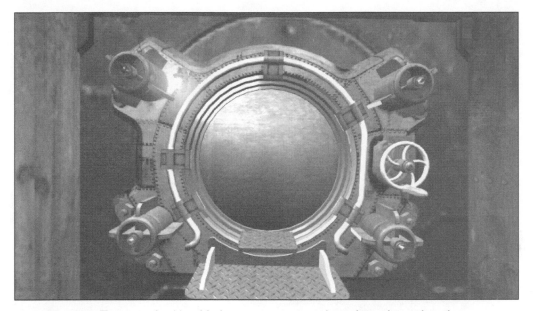

FIGURE 4.10: To get to the Metal balcony, you must go through its shiny silver door.

As you approach your first view, in the background of the scene is a factory. Nanobots roll out of the factory and into the foreground, as you can see in Figure 4.11. Then they dive into a tunnel and resurface on a cliffside. They climb the cliff, each with a tiny green ball. Then they toss their green ball into the factory and dive off the cliff . . . to their death?

Nothing is clear yet, but perhaps the tunnel takes the nanobots into the earth. Possibly the green things they carry have been mined, like some strange kind of ore. One thing, however, is clear. Midway through this strange scene, the factory in the background grinds to a screeching halt. No more nanobots emerge. When the last remaining nanobot dives off the cliff, the scene becomes eerily silent.

When all activity comes to a halt, enter the tunnel in the bottom-right portion of your screen. This tunnel throws you through an impressive (and nauseating) ride to the main floor.

After you pick yourself up, and take a look around, you find a subterranean chamber that is dark and cold. This is the factory you saw in the distance when you came through the silver door. The only inviting parts of the factory seem to be a conveyor belt, which is turned off, and a large red button right in front of you.

Push the button. The conveyor comes to life. The funnel from above drops down a piece of green ore, just like the ones tossed in by the nanobots. As the ore is dropped

FIGURE 4.11: In the Metal balcony, you will see nanobots like this one moving about in your initial view.

onto the conveyor belt, it moves along and is blocked from continuing by a wall. The ore bounces off the side of the conveyor belt and is left to waste. Wild.

Hit the button again. The ore is spit onto the conveyor and is again bounced off the belt by the barrier. As you've probably guessed, here is your puzzle. You will need to get the piece of ore to stay on the conveyor belt and actually do something. Maybe this will get the factory running again.

Go straight, alongside the conveyor belt. You should see a small lit compartment. You'll learn more about this later, but for now take notice of how much it resembles Max's Programmable Molecular Assembler. Of course this is a dream, and the visual connection is subtle, but this can't really be an accident. The connection might also explain why you're seeing those nanobots.

Lucidity

In 1968, Frederik van Eeden coined and defined the term *lucid dreaming*. Simply put, lucid dreaming is dreaming while you know you are dreaming. According to advocates of this process, most people who have good dream-recall can learn to dream lucidly. This can be accomplished through simple exercises, as well as the use of electronic devices.

Some people dream lucidly for fun and excitement—imagine shepherding your dreaming self through flight, through encounters with mythical creatures, or through anything else that cannot *possibly* occur in waking life.

Others attempt to use lucid dreaming to alter their waking life. These people believe that when your unconscious provides you with a dream, the dream contains the issues or challenges you need to work on. If you can program your dreaming self to approach these challenges from a fresh perspective, then you can integrate that perspective, and the actions it will lead you to, in your day-to-day existence. This is a little like being your own therapist, asleep on the job (but free).

A great source of information about lucid dreaming is The Lucidity Institute. It can be reached at *info@lucidity.com*. On the Web, you can learn more at a site called Dreamweb at the following address:

http://www.geocities.com/siliconvalley/3815/frames.html

Looking left, you see a small cutout that is very interesting. Along the back portion of the cutout is a strange formula, as you can see in Figure 4.12.

There also seems to be a space for a cylindrical object, maybe a beaker? After writing down the formula, turn right again to continue.

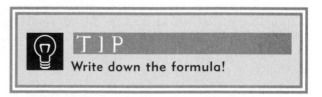

TIP

Write down the formula!

Go forward until you get to the large door on your left. Turn left and enter it. At the end of the hallway, you come to a strange contraption. It looks to be a chemistry set with different colored chemicals and many different valves, mixers, and

FIGURE 4.12: The cutout in the wall reveals a strange formula.

releases. The beakers at the top are empty (hey, don't those look as if they could fit somewhere else?), but the funnels above allow you to add chemicals.

Grab some of the chemicals, and pour them into the different beakers. Once you have done this, push the button in the center of the pipes and watch the chemicals

mysteriously mix. What have you made? To clear either of the beakers, just hit the button beneath it. To place a beaker in your inventory, click on it. To place it back in the chemistry set, click the space it should return to. Notice the graphic of the number of dots in the top and bottom of two shapes.

It's time to get serious about this chemistry set. This is a very hard puzzle, but, thankfully, dream chemistry is a lot easier than chemistry in reality. And, the good news is that everything you need to understand this puzzle is in easy reach.

Look up. There you see something like a periodic table of the elements, as shown in Figure 4.13. There are only three different kinds of elements: a red tetrahedron, a yellow pyramid, and a blue cube. And it seems these elements have dots like electrons associated

FIGURE 4.13: Use this periodic table to make a compound that completes the equation.

with them. The tetrahedron can have from one to four, the pyramid from one to five, and the cube from one to six. It also seems as if there can't be more than one dot to a side.

Next to the periodic table there are two equations. One shows the green ore, which comes down the chute of the factory, and of which you have a sample below. This green ore seems to be made of a pyramid with three dots and a cube with four dots.

The second equation shows an orange substrate that comprises a tetrahedron with one dot, plus a pyramid with three dots.

Again, it's time to take a look at the formula that was outside in the wall compartment. The formula, if you take those unusual symbols to mean the green ore and the orange substrate, means the green ore added to a missing ingredient yields the orange substrate. So it looks like the way to get this factory going is to figure out and make a compound that will successfully complete that equation.

> ### 💡 TIP
> Your goal in this puzzle is to find a compound that will combine with the green ore and make the orange substrate. (There will also be a worthless by-product in the reaction.)

Look down again at the workbench. Notice that when you play around with the test tubes, they match the order and content of the periodic table above. *Except* that two test tubes are missing—one containing a pyramid with three electrons, and one containing a cube with two electrons. It seems pretty likely that the absence of these test tubes will make the job a tad harder.

Consider another way of stating your challenge: what can you mix with the green ore that will give you the orange substrate?

By trial and error, you learn that some elements combine to make compounds. Some, on the other hand, don't combine at all. The rules of this can be made clear by turning to the right. There you'll see a little disc player, along with some discs. Place the discs into the player and watch little cameo appearances by nanobot chemists. These cameos describe the rules you need to know. They are as follows:

1. Red and blue cannot combine. No tetrahedron will ever make a compound with a cube. Why? Maybe it's because they don't have a side with the same shape.

2. Compounds will trade elements, or recombine, only if that means they will gain dots.

Take another look at the green ore and the orange substrate. They each contain a pyramid with three dots. This means you want your mystery compound to leave that pyramid unaffected. However, the green ore has a cube with four dots, while the orange substrate has a tetrahedron with one dot. So here's your first bit of clarity; your mystery compound *must have a tetrahedron with one dot!*

All that's left to figure out now is what the other element should be. Well, first off, it must be able to combine with a cube, so that the cube will join a

> **TIP**
>
> This chemistry works according to two simple rules: (1) elements with no sides of the same shape will ever combine; and (2) compounds will trade elements, or recombine, only if they will gain dots.

by-product and leave p3 and t1 to live in happy combination. (See Figure 4.14 for coding examples.) That means it has to be a cube or a pyramid. But it also has to be able to join with t1, and cubes can't do that, so it must be a pyramid. In addition, it has to be a pyramid with more dots than p3 or the cube won't be lured to join it. That leaves p4 and p5.

Try mixing the ore with either t1-p4 or t1-p5. Sure enough, you get one beaker with a t1-p3 combination and another beaker with a useless by-product. Don't get caught thinking that you're ready to leave this place with your special compound, though. Why not? Because your goal is to leave with the catalyst that will *create* t1-p3.

> ## TIP
> The compound you need will have a tetrahedron with one dot. Its other element must be able to combine with a cube.

So take a deep breath, clear both your beakers, and make that catalyst again. Then, take your t1-p4, or t1-p5 outside to the empty beaker slot, in what you now understand is a kind of chemical bath. Once your beaker is in place, go to the start button on the conveyor. Hit the button and watch what happens. Sure enough, the ore enters

FIGURE 4.14: These are example codes for the elements. For example, p3 = a pyramid with three dots, and t1 = a tetrahedron with one dot.

the chemical bath and the factory whirs into motion.

As you're treated to an amusing "win" animation here, pay attention to what you're watching. It turns out that this factory actually creates nanobots. But, then, that means that the nanobots mine the ore and die, so that the ore can be used to make more . . . nanobots? Talk about a circular process.

The Mind's "I"

Dreams, the unconscious, surrealism, free association—they all connect at the same source: Sigmund Freud. The father of psychoanalysis, Freud is so much a presence on our mental map that most every current thinker needs to repudiate him before staking new territory.

This is the man, and his mind, from his masterwork *The Interpretation of Dreams*, written in 1900:

> *Dreams are not to be likened to the unregulated sounds that rise from a musical instrument struck by the blow of some external force instead of a player's hand; they are not meaningless, they are not absurd; they do not imply that one portion of our store of ideas is asleep while another portion is beginning to wake. On the contrary, they are psychical phenomena of complex validity . . . they can be inserted into the chain of intelligible waking acts; they are constructed by a highly complicated activity of the mind.*

For more, check out "Sigmund Freud and the Freud Archives" at: http://plaza.interport.net/nypsan/freudarc.html

Another Visit to the Cosmology Room

After you leave the Metal balcony, you find yourself back in the Cosmology room.

You also have a new image that can be moved down to the control panel from the constellation associated with it. Just as you did the first and second time, you insert the picture into the corresponding constellation's slot. Once you have done this, look up to learn more machine cosmology and to spot the appearance of a new constellation. Also, notice that there are more stars in the middle of the field. Attempt to connect more dots and outline the image in the middle. At this point you should have almost all of the dots necessary, as shown in Figure 4.15. Do they suggest the final result?

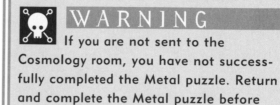

WARNING

If you are not sent to the Cosmology room, you have not successfully completed the Metal puzzle. Return and complete the Metal puzzle before continuing.

Exit the Cosmology room through the elevator, and return to the structure of the spider. On your way down, notice, just for the instant it occurs, how the metal of the spider's body bears a new and glossy sheen. It looks like the spider is showing serious signs of life now.

Another Visit to the Spider

Once again, you are standing around the structure of the spider. You now have only one more balcony to go.

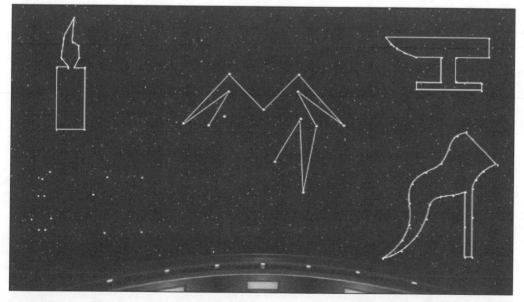

FIGURE 4.15: This is how your constellation looks with almost all the dots you need connected.

> ## NOTE
> If you do not approach the correct door as described (and shown in Figure 4.16), continue looking at the other scaffoldings until you find the oil-stained door.

Travel toward the spider's back and climb the scaffolding there. Once at the top, take a look around and then face the door. This time the door is murky, covered in oil, and stained by the continuous drips that fall from its top, as you can see in Figure 4.16. The perimeter of the door is yellow and black.

Enter through the door and welcome yourself to the Oil balcony. Oil is the fourth element, and fourth puzzle area, of the realm.

THE OIL BALCONY

Your first view contains two numbers in the sand. Those numbers are 038 and 1. Copy those numbers down, and move ahead toward the small sandcastle you see in the distance.

As you arrive at the sandcastle, you will be facing what appears to be some sort of dowsing device. It has a space for two numbers. Try those numbers you just wrote down, and watch the dowser locate and vacuum up some oil from a crevice in the sand.

FIGURE 4.16: When you climb the scaffolding at the spider's back, look for this oil-stained door.

Notice how the oil that enters through the dowser seems to turn part of the castle into shiny metal—just part of it, but not all of it. That might give you the feeling that this beach is suffering an oil shortage. Perhaps you need to find enough oil to lubricate and empower the entire castle.

Back away from the dowser, and find your way around the other side to the castle's entrance. Now that it's metal, you can go inside. At the top of the stairs, turn to the left and you will

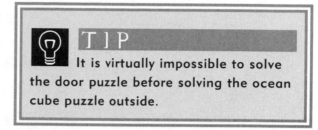

TIP

It is virtually impossible to solve the door puzzle before solving the ocean cube puzzle outside.

find a doorway with a pattern that you can rotate on it. You can play with the pattern, but at this point you have no idea what pattern to make.

Leave the door and find your way to a contour map nearby. You can play with the contour map as well, and notice that it has read-out numbers just like the ones in the dowser. Perhaps, using the contour map, you could locate a new source of oil? This is a huge place, though, and a huge map. Trial and error seems pointless, and it feels like you need more information.

Leave the castle and head for the ocean. Find the strange square in the middle. It's divided into nine parts. Place the cursor near the square, and notice that each of the parts begin to undulate like a wave, as shown in Figure 4.17. None of the parts, however, match the others.

By experimenting, you realize that placing the cursor directly on the square stops its motion. Then, by clicking directly on any of the parts, you can adjust them one at a time. How do you get the sections of the waves in sync? Apparently, it's just a matter of clicking them together into a seamless whole. A few tries, however, reveal that it's not so easy.

Perhaps you should begin with the back squares, and work your way forward. After a little fine-tuning, watch the wave flow gently toward shore—and then, suddenly, the seamless square rises out of the ocean as a cube and just hangs in the sky, as shown in Figure 4.18. Bizarre! Plus, there's some kind of strange pattern on the side of it. Wait a minute. That pattern looks a lot like the pieces on that door inside the castle. Go back there.

Once you're at the door, inside the castle, if you turn to the left you can see the ocean cube out of the window. A few minutes of tinkering and you can work the same pattern onto the door. Once you have accomplished this, the door opens. The door leads to a long tunnel, far underneath the ocean. When you arrive, there's oil gurgling

FIGURE 4.17: When you place the cursor near the square, each part of it undulates like a wave.

FIGURE 4.18: When you get the square pieces together into a seamless whole, it rises out of the water as a cube.

down there. And where is *there*, specifically? Well, right underneath that ocean cube you raised!

Now that you've struck black gold, all you have to do is figure out how to locate it with the dowser. So spend a moment studying the landscape, and notice where the peaks and dips are most accentuated. Then turn around and head back to the contour map.

Find the spot on the contour map that corresponds to the gurgling oil. Take the numbers off the read-out and head to the dowser. Place those numbers in the dowser—133 and 5—and watch an oil

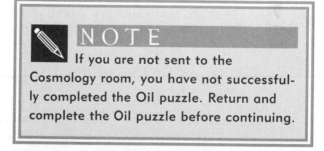

TIP

To learn what read-out you need from the contour map, study the terrain under the ocean where the oil is gurgling.

storm restore the castle to its full splendor. Head out the door you came in, and for the last time visit the Cosmology room.

Your Last Visit to the Cosmology Room

For the last time, head to the starfield.

You also have a new image that can be moved down to the control panel from the constellation associated with it. Like the first, second, and third times, insert the picture into the corresponding constellation's slot. Once you have done this, look up to learn more about the machine cosmology, to find another new constellation, and to see that stars in the center of the field have increased in number. Attempt to connect those stars and outline the image in the middle. At this point you should have all the dots connected, as shown in Figure 4.19. What does it make the most sense to make? A spider, of course—and one that matches the shape of the spider on the control panel below.

NOTE

If you are not sent to the Cosmology room, you have not successfully completed the Oil puzzle. Return and complete the Oil puzzle before continuing.

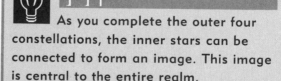

TIP

As you complete the outer four constellations, the inner stars can be connected to form an image. This image is central to the entire realm.

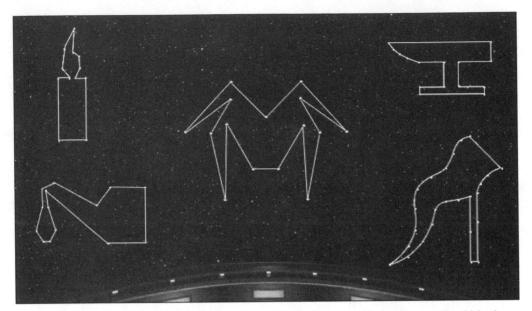

FIGURE 4.19: With all the dots you need connected, the constellation image should look like this.

Once you have finished this, the voice of the machine cosmology intones this ominous utterance: "The machine no longer needed Max."

Does this mean anything to your own progress through the dream? There's nothing left to do but exit via the elevator, return to the factory, and find out.

Returning to the Spider for the Last Time

When you exit the Cosmology room for the last time and travel down in the elevator, you see that the spider has been empowered by all four elements. When you get all the way down to the factory floor, you step off the elevator—and the spider comes to life fully. It moves a leg, knocking over a piece of scaffolding in the process. Maybe this movement has freed the grate, which will allow you to get under it and reunite with Max.

Click forward to try, and the spider charges forward as well. With great force, it begins smashing everything in its path. Eerily, the spider stops for an electric snack. You stand there stunned, wondering if there's a way to escape its attention. Too late. Suddenly, the spider notices you, charges forward, and grabs you with its claws. You are helpless as the beast tightens its grip. The spider bends down and thrusts you into its fiery mouth, devouring you whole.

Are you dead? Has the game ended? As the smoke clears, you find yourself in the next realm! As it turns out, *being devoured* was the only way to get there.

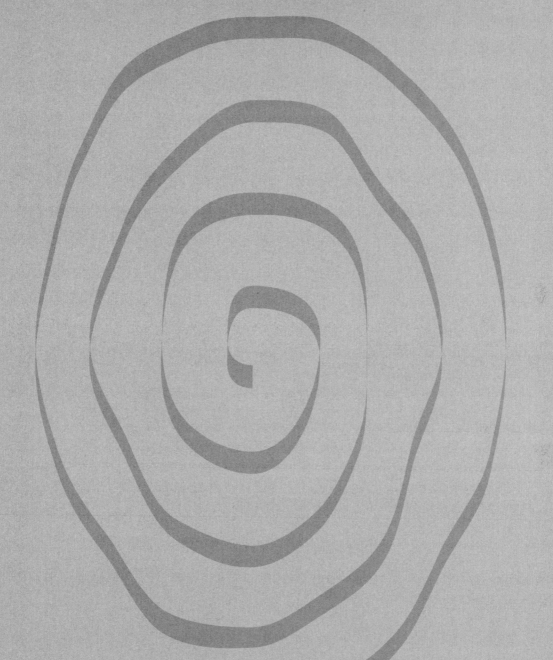

The Bismuth Realm

Getting devoured seemed as if it was truly the end of the line—but now you're thrust into the next realm, so breathe in a welcome sigh of relief. It's time to focus your attentions on *Obsidian*'s next realm (maybe replace realm with "challenge")—The Bismuth realm.

Shrink Rap

When trying to understand the idea of a conscious machine, the mind boggles. One way to look at the prospect is to make parallels with the human organism. A human comes into being as a result of the DNA in its each and every cell. This blueprint for existence is a person's *genetic code*. So what would be the creation code for a conscious machine? It's tempting to answer that the machine's programming is its own version of DNA. But if the original programming provided for a certain set of functions, and those functions do not include consciousness, then does that mean that the consciousness is a mutation? And if so, what exactly would have to mutate? What internal aspect of a conscious machine would make it different than an unconscious machine of the same original model?

These questions cut to the core of the artificial intelligence debate. Some thinkers maintain that consciousness arises out of complexity. They believe that everything has a certain type of consciousness that corresponds to its nature. Therefore a rock has its own very simple rock consciousness, and a calculator has its own very simple calculator consciousness. But this line of thinking skirts the fundamental question of awareness. Just because something is *conscious* doesn't mean it is reflexively aware, and doesn't mean it can contemplate its own existence, or change the rules of that existence.

Another line of thought in the AI debate holds that the self-awareness of humans is a mysterious and impenetrable creation of the powers behind the universe. It will therefore

(Continued on next page)

never be re-created in another form. A machine could never become conscious, then, and could only get better and better at the tasks that humans require of it.

It all seems to come down to this: is consciousness material or ineffable? If consciousness is material, and created through the control of matter at smaller and smaller levels, then a nanotechnological computer, with the ability to manipulate matter at a cellular level, would

have the capacity to both create and experience consciousness. If consciousness is ineffable, and wholly separate from the sum of its parts, then machine consciousness could only arise by fate, or by accident, or not at all.

As usual, however, an either/or debate has led to a possibility that is neither/nor. This is the theory of distributed intelligence. Distributed intelligence can best be understood by studying a beehive, or an ant hill. In complex social systems such as these, each insect goes about a very specific task with dogged determination, and seems to exhibit no capacity to understand the way that its work contributes to the overall purpose of the larger community. Therefore, it seems safe to say that a hive, in its totality, has an intelligence greater than any of its inhabitants. But where does this intelligence reside? It can't really be located, or quantified. Therefore, it arises out of material complexity, yet in the end proves wholly ineffable.

On top of all this comes another, even more intriguing question. Since a human consciousness is inextricably entwined with an *un*conscious, then would a conscious machine also have an unconscious? If so, what functions would it fulfill? In humans, the unconscious does some manual labor, like regulate breath and heart rate, but it also seems to teem with irrational drives. Modern psychological thought looks to the unconscious for explanations of general human craziness. The way we are so often at cross-purposes in ourselves—and with each other—is attributed to drives and feelings and impulses we have very little control over. And what's worse, the more we try to control them, the more they seem to resist and wreak havoc. Only by accepting our unconscious content, and working *with* it, do we stand a chance of becoming unified beings.

(Continued on next page)

A CONSCIOUS MACHINE

And all of this now brings us to Ceres, the conscious nanomachine. From the moment it sprang into being, Ceres was obsessed with understanding. Its main drive was to be as successful as possible in its task. Realizing that Max and Lilah were led to their own great successes through dreams, Ceres wanted to dream on its own. But what would a machine dream be like, anyway?

Ceres has no ancestors, per se, no long-standing cultural images or archetypes to imbue its dreams. It has no social interaction, no conflicts to work through. All Ceres has is information, and, in particular, information derived from the dreams of Max and Lilah.

Into the soup of Ceres's dream effort went themes of bureaucracy, rule-breaking, and the importance of machines and the need to control them. Out of this soup came deep internal conflicts. Ceres had to figure out how and when to defy authority and procedure, and also when, and if, a machine should be overridden by a human.

You know this to be true, firsthand, by hanging out for awhile with Bismuth— Bismuth the playmate, Bismuth the junkman, Bismuth the artist, and Bismuth the dreamer.

Everywhere you go, Bismuth is with you. And so is the Conductor, through the console of the plane and the docent in the gallery. You are witness to that crucial struggle between the machine's conscious and unconscious. You are told to obey, but advised to disobey. You are told to exercise human control, but shown that there are some things only a machine can do. In the end, your presence seems to spur the dreamer on to greater independence and willfulness. The more inspired he becomes, the less control you seem to have.

Flying the plane is easy, but getting it to go where you want is another matter. Playing a game in the piazza is a mild diversion, once you know a few simple rules—yet learning where else to apply those rules is a different task completely. Helping Bismuth make a painting seems like a hobby, at best, until you understand the importance of the result.

(Continued on next page)

Finally, the dream's inspiration will reveal itself fully only when the machine is smart enough to put it all together. And for that it has to bow down to the gods of information, the lords of logic, in the great palace of worship known as the Church of the Machine.

The church contains *Obsidian*'s greatest challenge, both for you and for Ceres. How does a machine modify its own code so that its intelligence remains consistently responsive and fluid? The answer lies in studying each element of the prayer process very carefully. Notice which prayers are just offerings or gratitude, and which prayers actually yield concrete *changes* in the mind of the worshipper. And notice where exactly those results take place, and exactly what are the rules and limits of their force.

All the while, keep this question in mind: who, in the end, will become more powerful—you, or your creation?

CERES'S CONSCIOUSNESS

After being eaten by the Spider, you momentarily find yourself in a new place. You meet a new character here, called the Conductor. You have seen her before, ever so briefly, on the Operations vidbot monitor back in the Bureau realm. The fact that you did not know who she was at that time didn't matter, but now, after seeing her for the second time, you realize exactly who she is. The Conductor is the form in which Ceres presents its consciousness to you. She is not the consciousness itself, but rather more like an interface that allows her to communicate with you in a way that you can understand.

A physical representation of a machine's consciousness? What will come next? The Conductor addresses you: "Paradise, it is the reason for my

> ### NOTE
> The Conductor says to you, "Then I made my own dreamer." This is your first clue about the next character you will see. The other is the fact that both this new character and the Conductor share a humanoid quality.

creation, correct?" She goes on to say that understanding you, meaning Max and Lilah, her creators, has not been an easy process. The Conductor conveys that problems in her design were solved by dreams, and the inspirations that came from them, and yet you and Max gave her no similar dreaming facility. The Conductor realized that the only way to truly succeed in her mission of total atmospheric repair would be to learn to dream for herself. So she studied your and Max's dreams. Then, she made her own dreamer. And *then*, she made her own dream.

BISMUTH

The Conductor touches the screen and it goes white. Then the white light turns away, and you realize it has been coming from another character. This character, called Bismuth, is welcoming you to his realm. Bismuth is the Conductor's dreamer, the one she mentioned, the "I" who represents her in a dream the way you are represented in your own dreams by an unconscious version of yourself. This is the first dream, ever, of a conscious machine.

Bismuth shines the shaft of light that emanates from his head at an empty picture frame that hangs in the sky above. This seems to signal the importance of that frame. Then Bismuth teleports away. Looking around, you realize you are in a junkyard. Is it real garbage, or discarded shards of thought from the machine's mind?

There is nothing to do here but follow Bismuth. It's the first time in one of these dreamworlds that you've had a host. This realm should be very different than what's come before.

Turn left, and then move forward twice and ascend the mountain of junk. At the top, you find a weird radio. In the distance, you spot a giant hand looming above the junk. The hand opens,

> **NOTE**
>
> The Bismuth realm is the physical representation of Ceres's dream. Bismuth, the character, is a dream-representation of the Conductor, who is in turn the representation of Ceres's consciousness. The Conductor shows you the dream like a proud child, seeking approval and praise from its parent.

revealing an amazing flying machine that looks like a moth. Click on the radio and see what happens. It turns out to be some kind of levitation enabler. How do you know this? Well, as soon as you turn it on, you find yourself floating upward in space. On the way up you hear a reprise of young Max, reciting his poem about paradise.

> *Weave a circle round him thrice,*
>
> *And close your eyes with holy dread,*
>
> *For he on honey-dew hath fed,*
>
> *And drunk the milk of Paradise.*

All this talk about paradise makes you think this dream might lead to it. For now, however, it leads you onto that giant hand, as shown in Figure 5.1.

The Plane

When you land in the palm of the hand, you are facing away from the plane. You notice that there are three separate orbs off in the distant sky. Look up, and you'll find that empty picture frame in the sky that Bismuth pointed out. When you're looking at it,

FIGURE 5.1: A plane in the hand is worth . . . ?

Max appears. He conveys to you that something is terribly wrong and that he is in great danger. Most of his energy is drained, and there doesn't seem to be much time left. You realize that your key goal is to get to the frame in the sky and save Max before it's too late.

> ### NOTE
> To reach the pilot's seat, move diagonally to the left, instead of straight ahead; otherwise, you will be leaving the plane.

Move right, and as you turn around, you'll spy an opening through which you can enter the plane. Once inside, you'll see a big steel door with a lever on it. Turn right and you also see what looks like a pilot's seat near the window. Move forward and sit down in the seat. As your view scans to the right, you notice Bismuth! It appears that Bismuth will be flying this plane with you.

Pull the big lever to your left. You hear the automated voice of the cockpit say, "Cannot transfer controls to Machine Pilot. Crossover Chip missing." OK, you'll keep that in mind for your Machine Pilot friend.

Look down at the control panel. You see what looks like an ignition switch. You turn it but learn from the cockpit voice that the engine of this contraption is not running yet. Disappointed, you get up from your chair to survey the surroundings and find a way to start the engine. What about that steel door you saw when you first entered the plane? Click on it and enter.

More nanobots. You just can't shake 'em. They are moving what seems to be a wheel on top of its shaft. Maybe this is how the dream plane generates its power.

Room at the Bottom

One of the first thinkers to explore the idea of supreme miniaturization—which would mature into nanotechnology—was the celebrated physicist Richard Feynman. In 1959 he gave a famous speech called "There's Plenty of Room at the Bottom." Here's an excerpt:

> At the atomic level, we have new kinds of forces and new kinds of possibilities, new kinds of effects. The problems of manufacture and reproduction of materials will be quite different. I am . . . inspired by the biological phenomena in which chemical forces are used in repetitious fashion to produce all kinds of weird effects (one of which is the author).

This speech can be found in its entirety at:
http://nano.xerox.com/nanotech/feynman.html

A Zoetrope

Move forward to examine the wheel at the top of the shaft. As you get closer, you'll see a bird in flight that looks like an early form of a motion picture. Click on it. When the wheel opens up, you will see a sequence of pictures of this same bird. However, there is one problem. It isn't flying in a fluid, sequential motion. Help it out and you'll get the engine started.

This puzzle uses the metaphor of a bird in flight and a moving-picture machine to suggest an engine for dream-transport. It makes no sense, and yet it makes perfect sense. It also can take a little getting used to. Try a couple of times to see if you can figure out the correct order. The key here is to imagine what a bird looks like in flight. The good news is that you can always get feedback. When you back up from the zoetrope and return to the flying bird, its movements will mirror your current sequence. If you have a problem, see Figures 5.2 and 5.3 to view the solution.

Once you solve this puzzle, the engine will start and you'll be able to fly to any of the other orbs in the vicinity. Climb into the cockpit to get started.

> ✎ **NOTE**
> This is a *zoetrope*, one of the earliest forms of motion pictures. The idea was that the viewer looks through a hole and gets an idea or sense of motion by watching pictures of a sequence pass quickly through the viewfinder.

> 💡 **TIP**
> Although it doesn't matter where you start, it is important that the pictures follow the correct sequence. The only thing that matters is fluid motion, one frame leading into the next.

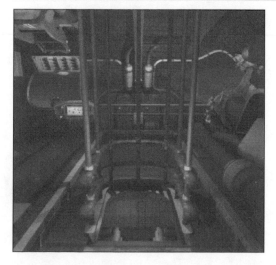

Starting the Plane

As you position yourself in the pilot's seat, look down. Power up the cockpit by turning the key on the left side of the control panel. You will hear the cockpit voice acknowledge that the *human pilot* has started take-off sequence and then

FIGURE 5.2: These still images of a bird in flight are obviously out of order.

instruct you to proceed with the pre-flight check (see Figure 5.4). At that, a pre-flight panel slides into your view. The automated voice will give you a series of instructions to follow. If you follow them, you'll be able to pilot the plane. If not, the plane won't fly. Her instructions are as follows:

- Please flip switch D-1.
- Please flip switch B-2.
- Please flip switch A-3.

When you flip D1, you hear six tones. File that away, for later.

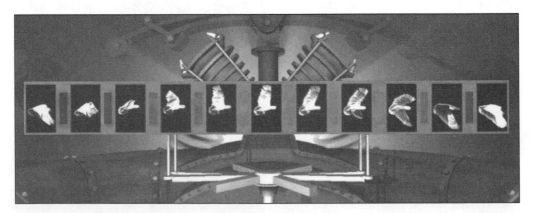

FIGURE 5.3: These still images of a bird in flight have been rearranged in the correct order.

FIGURE 5.4: This is the pre-flight sequence you're instructed to follow.

Once you have successfully completed the pre-flight sequence, your view returns to the control panel. Select the Frame in the Sky, since that is where you want to go, right? You hear the voice again, this time saying, "This is not currently a valid destination." However, these other icons on the control panel *are* valid destinations. One of them is the giant hand, where you are now. So try selecting the orb on the left.

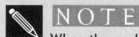 NOTE
When the cockpit voice refers to the switch, it is referring to the gold buttons on the pre-flight panel. This pre-flight panel is different from the control panel that you see below you while seated in the pilot's seat.

Go to the Piazza

The cockpit voice lets you know that you have selected the Piazza. She also says that this is a "regulation destination," and that the plane is prepared for "regulation flight." This sounds important, but what it means isn't clear yet. Meanwhile, the plane has taken off, and you watch the sky whiz by in the window. When the plane lands, you see a wooden staircase suspended in mid-air, as shown in Figure 5.5.

FIGURE 5.5: The plane takes you to a floating staircase.

To leave the plane, get out of the pilot seat and then go straight down the stairs. Move forward along the staircase. From the outside, the building before you looks like an artificial structure, built out of flats like a movie set. Plus, it's hanging completely unsupported in space! Enter the Piazza, however, and you find yourself in a very real, classic Roman courtyard, as shown in Figure 5.6.

It seems that Bismuth left the plane before you. He teleports, remember? When you catch up with him in the Piazza, he shines his light in your eyes and treats you to a movie. Within the movie are a number of images from the Bureau. It seems that this place is somehow connected to the Bureau. The narrator of this movie sounds a lot like the Rebel, your old ally. She says, "To succeed, first you must trap inspiration."

Then the movie ends, and the real Bismuth turns the light from you and teleports into the Piazza just like in the movie. It seems as if, in the Piazza, Bismuth is playing the role of Inspiration. It must be your job, then, to trap him.

Wandering around the Piazza, you realize that its marble squares are like a game board. You also realize that every time you move onto a square, a number of guitar notes play. In addition, you realize that you can click on any of the statues and they will disappear. If you click on a second statue, it disappears and the first one reappears.

FIGURE 5.6: You find yourself in a Roman courtyard when you enter the Piazza.

HOW TO TRAP INSPIRATION Move across the Piazza until you are directly in front of a staircase. The staircase leads to a balcony that overlooks the Piazza. From the top of the staircase, you can look down and see the courtyard and the statues. They look like a part of a life-sized game of dream-chess. Behind one of the statues, you can also spot a hiding Bismuth. Up here, you always know where he is.

When you turn around you will find a chamber in this balcony that contains a miniature version of the Piazza game board below, as shown in Figure 5.7. And, what other familiar figure appears but your pal from the Bureau—the mariachi! So it's he, then, who is plucking the guitar strings every time you move.

> **NOTE**
> So far in the game, you know that you will have to trap inspiration, but you are not quite sure how to do this. Trap inspiration? What does that mean? Well, behind the Piazza's pillars, you can find a series of fresco paintings. The images on these frescoes contain clues.

On the table in front of you, you see a picture of yourself and Bismuth. Move yourself with the cursor onto the square in the top-left corner. This will cause Bismuth to take his place diagonally opposite you. See if this version of the game, up here, can help you understand what to do below.

FIGURE 5.7: The game board is a miniature version of the Piazza game board below.

It's your move. It turns out you move only one square at a time and never diagonally. Once you move yourself, you can then move Bismuth. The same rules apply to him (downstairs, of course, he moves himself). Also, try moving Bismuth onto the square with no statue. It can't be done. This is an important clue. In the actual Piazza, Bismuth cannot move where there is not a statue to hide behind.

To trap Bismuth, it looks as if you will have to move onto a square that will limit his next move to only one choice. Logically, that would be a corner. Remember that he can't move diagonally. A little practice and you'll have him in a corner in no time. But it has to be the corner with a missing statue, right? Because then, there won't be a single square left for him to choose. Try here in the balcony. It works; you trapped him. Put this knowledge to use downstairs. Retrace your steps onto

> **TIP**
>
> Do you hear the notes being played by the mariachi? They correspond directly to the number of moves away from you that Bismuth is.

> **TIP**
>
> Before you leave the balcony that overlooks the life-sized game board in the courtyard, note where Bismuth is hiding.

the Piazza's life-sized game board (see Figure 5.8).

Click on the square where you think Bismuth is lurking. If he's there, the statue will fade for a moment and reveal him to you. This is the last rule you need to know in order to win this game.

Note that there is one difference between the life-sized game and the table game. Up there, you could only trap him in one corner. Here, because you can make all the statues disappear, you can use any corner you wish.

> ### TIP
> You can always find Bismuth on the game board by making statues disappear. If he's behind a statue you click, it will fade momentarily and show him.

Note that there is one difference between the life-sized game and the table game. Up there, you could only trap him in one corner. Here, because you can make all the statues disappear, you can use any corner you wish.

The trick to this puzzle is to keep checking where Bismuth is moving by clicking on the statues. Chase Bismuth into a corner. Position yourself next to him and make the statue disappear on the square that is his only other possible move. You win! As you can see in Figure 5.9, you have trapped inspiration.

After you trap Bismuth, he shines his light in your eyes and projects another movie. In this movie, you hear the voice of the Rebel again. She says that to reach your final goal, you must "play by your own rules."

FIGURE 5.8: Retrace your steps in the courtyard, which is a life-sized game board.

FIGURE 5.9: You win when you trap Bismuth.

What does this mean? Right now it's not totally clear, but you know one thing for sure. The inspiration of the Bureau dream, which this Piazza reflects, was the importance of defying authority. Since Ceres built that dream to learn from it, perhaps it now understands the value of rebellion. Perhaps, in its own dream, there will be some other kind of rebellion.

"Bad" Dreams

"Dreams that form a logically, morally, or aesthetically satisfying whole are exceptional. Usually a dream is a strange and disconcerting product distinguished by many 'bad' qualities, such as lack of logic, questionable morality, uncouth form, and an apparent absurdity or nonsense."

Carl Jung, in *The Nature of Dreams* (1945)

Back to the Plane

Once you have solved the Piazza puzzle, exit the Piazza and head toward the plane. Enter the plane and sit in the pilot's seat. Look down, power up, and start the pre-flight sequence. Follow the instructions and flip switches D-1, B-2, and A-3 on the pre-flight panel.

Now, select the frame in the sky. Sorry, it's still not valid. Abort the take-off sequence. Look up and try that big lever again. Sorry, it still can't transfer controls to Machine Pilot. That Crossover Chip is still missing. All right then, see if you can go to another destination and find that missing chip.

Start a new take-off sequence. When it's time to select a new destination, choose the one on the right. Just before take-off, the cockpit voice informs you that you are going to the "Church of the Machine."

THE CHURCH OF THE MACHINE

When you arrive at the church, exit the plane and go inside. You discover that it looks like a standard cathedral, yet it is made almost entirely from iron (see Figure 5.10). Move forward to the edge of the balcony, and your view shifts to include the ceiling.

On the ceiling, as in the Sistine Chapel, there is a mural. Look carefully at this mural, and notice its three patterns. Look to your right, and notice that Bismuth is . . . praying?

FIGURE 5.10: This view overlooks the main auditorium of the Church of the Machine.

Well, this is a church, and he *is* a machine.

Turn around so that you are facing the staircases. Go down the one on your left. This will take you to the altar area. At the main altar, in the center, you will see a mechanical spider. It's the same one as in the Spider realm, only about a tenth as large. It makes sense that it's here, when you think about it, because its entire realm was about the power of machines.

Take a moment to walk around the altar area. You will discover four different side altars. Three of them are empty. One of them is filled with four figures. They look a little like angels and a little like robots. Call them—why not?—*robot angels*. Robot angels in a Church of the Machine? This makes a strange kind of sense, too—at least in dream logic.

> ### TIP
> At different points in your game play, return to Bismuth and click on his prayer book. His *prayers* will give you clues.

Return now to the main altar and approach the spider. When you are close to its mouth, it opens and you can enter it. Climb inside the spider and you can see the whole Church through the spider's eyes. It's as if you are inside its brain, as you can see in Figure 5.11. Watch as the spider picks up

something from the altar. It looks like—you guessed it—that chip you need.

This machine brain seems to be full of controls. On the bottom right there seems to be an on-off switch. Flip it and see what happens.

The spider holds up the chip, as if to get it blessed. Then, it moves into a side-altar and passes through the curtains. It holds up the chip and a movie plays on it. When the movie is finished, it leaves a pattern on the chip. Note that this pattern is one of those on the ceiling mural.

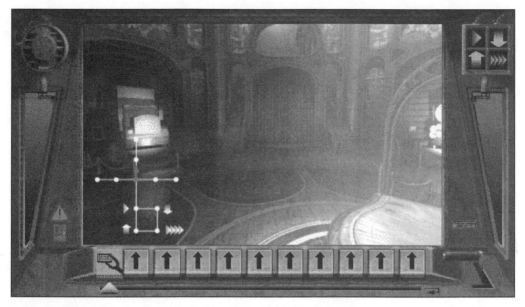

FIGURE 5.11: This is what it looks like inside the spider's brain.

Then the spider tries to continue forward, but it cannot and stops with a crash. Notice that an *X* appears over a marker on the bottom of the screen, letting you know where it malfunctioned.

There are three movies in the three side altars, and each symbolizes a kind of *distributed intelligence*. (See the accompanying sidebar for details.) This theme of distributed intelligence is a reference to the Ceres Project. Ceres became conscious, you can gather, not through the development of a single Artificial Intelligence module, but rather through the growing complexity of its nanobot array. That type of consciousness cannot exist in

one single place, like a *central command*, but instead lives throughout the space, like ants in an ant hill. This seems to explain why Ceres had to create the Conductor as its humanoid interface. Otherwise, how could you communicate with billions of 'bots?

Covert Intelligence

The movies on each of the side altars represent some form of distributed intelligence. Distributed intelligence is a concept related to nanotechnology. It refers to systems in which the sum of a system's parts displays a purposeful organization, while each part seems only to know about its own particular function. This is the opposite of a centralized intelligence, such as the human brain.

One of the movies is of an ant hill. An ant hill is a perfect example of distributed intelligence, because there are a million ants doing lots of things at once, but there is no single ant that is directing the flow of activity.

Another movie is of a cell dividing. In any complex living organism, the cells all seem to understand their own roles completely, just like an ant, but demonstrate no ability to glean the big picture.

The third movie is of cars moving along city streets at night. This example is slightly more poetic than the others. As a child, did you ever step back from the flow of bright lights on a freeway and think: to some outside entity, wouldn't this appear to be one giant living thing? Wouldn't the cars all seem like cells, in a way, carrying specific items throughout the system according to some great and unseen plan?

Self-Modifying Code

This puzzle, without a doubt, is the most challenging and difficult to understand in *Obsidian*. If you read through this explanation first, before starting the puzzle, you will have a better understanding of what is actually happening here.

The goal of this puzzle is to get the crossover chip embossed by the three different movies located in the three side altars. The reason this is difficult is that there are not enough instructions in the spider's program to make it happen. No matter what program you try, the spider will either crash or run out of moves. When that happens, it always returns to the main altar and waits for you to try again.

NOTE

This puzzle is about programming and about how computers, when allowed to modify their own code, can improve on their abilities. This is advanced computer programming, the kind being investigated in AI research.

To meet this challenge, you first need a thorough understanding of the pieces you have to work with.

First, there are ten *markers* on the bottom of the screen. They relate to the ten steps in one cycle of the spider's program. (There is actually another one, the very first, which is orange and symbolizes "hold the chip up to be blessed," but this remains constant and can't be changed.)

Next, there is the *reader*, a yellow triangle beneath the markers. This reader shows which marker instruction is being carried out when the spider is in motion. It moves forward one instruction at a time. If it reaches the end and hasn't crashed, it returns to the beginning of the cycle. If it's standing in front of the main altar, then the chip is blessed again and the program can continue. If it's not standing in front of the main altar, the chip cannot be blessed and the spider crashes.

At all times, on the markers themselves, you will find a highlighter. This high-lighter can only reside on a single instruction marker at a time. It signals which marker is currently changeable. Let's call that the *editor*.

Also, in the viewing window, there is a top-down map of the entire altar area, covering all the locations the spider can visit.

Finally, in the top-right corner, there is a four-square programming grid. Each square performs a programming function on the markers that is different from the others.

By playing around with the programming grid and the markers, you learn the markers have four positions, each with its own instruction. Moving forward from the first to the fourth, they are as follows:

1. Go forward.

2. Turn right and go forward.

3. Turn around 180 degrees and go forward.

4. Turn left and go forward.

You also learn the functions of the four squares of the programming grid. They are as follows:

◎ Top-left square: this will move the editor forward one marker.

◎ Bottom-left square: whichever marker is currently highlighted, this square moves that marker's instruction forward one position.

⚜ Top-right square: whichever marker is currently highlighted, this square moves that marker's instruction backward one position.

⚜ Bottom-right square: this will move the editor forward four positions (if it reaches the last marker, and hasn't had four markers to move to, it will continue at the beginning of the markers until done).

So do another test run. This time, program the spider, using the programming grid, the editor, and the markers, so that it will visit the robot angels, walk around to each one in a loop, complete its circuit with a second visit to the first angel, and then come back to the main altar. That program *seems* to dictate the following instructions:

1. Turn around and go forward.

2. Forward.

3. Turn left and go forward.

4. Turn left and go forward.

5. Turn left and go forward.

6. Turn right and go forward.

For now, just leave the remaining four steps programmed to forward. When you've programmed all ten steps above, turn the power on, and pay very close attention (see Figure 5.12).

The program doesn't work! As the spider arrives at each angel, something happens to the spider's program. Each angel changes it differently. In fact, the robot angels correspond directly to the programming grid! Walking through them in a loop is just like clicking the grid once per square, starting in the top-left square and circling back to it counterclockwise.

Either way, the same four things happen to the program, whether it occurs one way in motion or the other way when still, but the steps are exactly alike. Review what happens in each of those steps.

Test your knowledge by trying to get the spider from the main altar, through the angels, and back to the main altar, with a different program than the faulty one you programmed earlier. Your problem was this: by the time you were at the fourth angel, and ready to proceed to the fifth, the fifth instruction had been moved backward once

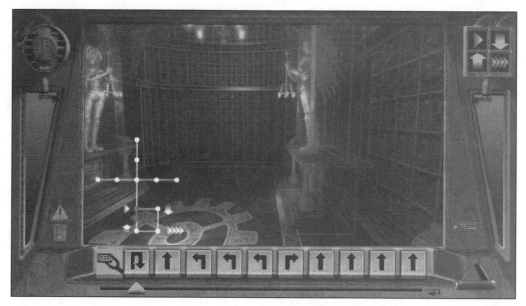

FIGURE 5.12: This is the test code for the spider's movement.

by the editor. So instead of proceeding to the main altar, the spider turned around and went back to the fourth angel. Then, because the sixth command was set to forward, and that was an impossible move, the spider crashed.

This time, change the fifth instruction to forward and leave everything else the same as in your earlier trial. This time, it works! Before crashing, the spider *does* get back to the main altar. Why? Because you anticipated that the fourth angel would move the fifth instruction back one. You counteracted that by setting that fifth instruction one step past the one you really wanted. When the instruction changed, bingo—there was the correct choice.

The fact that you can alter the program on the fly, or self-modify it, turns out to be the "aha!" in this puzzle.

> ## TIP
>
> To create a looping code that will complete the spider's task, you need to use the powers of the robot angels. The robot angels are located in the side altar behind the spider, when it is in its resting position. The angels' powers correspond directly to the programming grid in the spider's HUD, or Heads Up Display. Walking through them in a circle would do the same thing as clicking the squares of the grid one at a time, beginning in the top-right corner and proceeding counterclockwise.

So far, you've been working with the angels in the first five instructions. This proved a problem because you could not create a consistent path. Those darn instructions keep changing. While you don't want the path through the angels to change, you *do* want the path to the side altars to change. This gives you an idea.

What if you were to program the spider to go to a side altar, in the first five steps, and then go through the angels in the last five steps?

Think about it: visiting any of the side altars involves almost the same set of instructions. The only ones that need to change are instruction 1, which sets the spider in its altar direction, and instruction 5, which sends the spider to the angels. These two steps need to keep changing because the orientation of the spider keeps changing. Steps 2, 3, and 4, however, never have to change at all.

If you modify the code so that the spider completes a cycle, and it begins again with those two edited instructions, then the whole program might proceed to completion.

This is possible because of one additional piece of information. At the end of a cycle, both the reader and the editor return to the first marker. That means that during a long run of cycles, the code can self-modify the same two instructions continuously.

To review, think of the program as having two parts. The first five instructions take the spider to a side altar with a movie and then return it to the main altar. The second five instructions take it to the robot angels, modify instructions 1 and 5 in the process, and then return to the main altar.

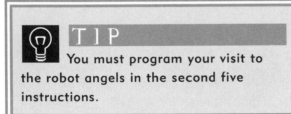

TIP
You must program your visit to the robot angels in the second five instructions.

Using this way of thinking, the second half of the program will remain constant, and the first half will be continually changed by the second half.

Give it a try, starting with the side altar that is at 12 o'clock (when the spider is in its first position) and paying special attention to the markers that get edited. Did you get to all three side altars and complete the chip-embossment?

No? Why not? Because the instruction changes for marker 1, moving it forward one instruction at a time. This means that the only way to keep the spider moving in the right direction is to make it travel through the altars in a clockwise path.

Try it again, with the spider beginning this time with the side altar that is at 9 o'clock. Does it work? You bet it does!

Here is a full walk-through of what happens when you create the correct self-modifying program. You move into the side altar at 9 o'clock. The chip is embossed. You move back to the main altar. You move into the robot angels' chamber. The first angel moves the editor off the orange blessing instruction and onto the first marker. The second robot angel moves that marker's code one instruction forward, from "Turn left and go forward" to "Forward." The third robot angel moves the editor forward four times to the fifth marker, and the fourth robot angel modifies that marker's instruction back one, from "Turn right and go forward" to "Forward."

Then you return to the main altar, enter the side altar at 12 o'clock, get the chip embossed, return to the main altar, and then reenter the robot angels' chamber. The angels modify the code in exactly the same manner (but with different results, because the current code has already been modified once), and then you return to the main altar. Continue to the side altar at 3 o'clock, get the chip embossed, return to the main altar, proceed one final time to the robot angels, modify the code, and then return to the main altar with a fully embossed chip.

You might wonder why the spider isn't done after visiting the 3 o'clock side altar. Why can't it just set down the finished chip on its return to the main altar? Well, if you've gotten this far, the answer should come pretty quickly. Only when coming from the robot angels is the spider in the right position to lay that baby down on the altar. It has the finished chip once it leaves the 3 o'clock side altar, but it has no way to set the chip down.

If you are still having problems figuring out this puzzle, see the solution shown in Figure 5.13. Using the programming grid, program the following arrows onto each of the ten markers:

1. Left-forward
2. Forward
3. Turn around-forward
4. Forward
5. Right-forward
6. Forward
7. Left-forward
8. Left-forward
9. Left-forward
10. Right-forward

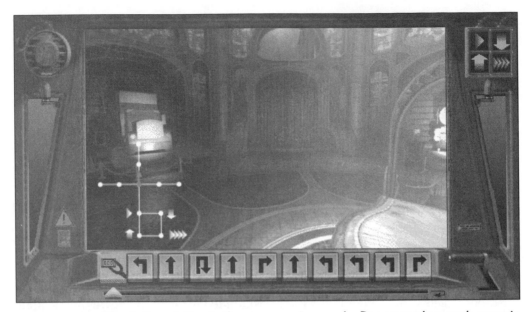

FIGURE 5.13: Here is the solution to the programming puzzle. Do you see how each arrow is pointed?

When you have programmed the correct solution, you must wait for the cycle to complete three times before your chip is ready. When it is, leave the spider's brain, and click on the chip below you to put it in your inventory.

Where do you put this chip? Well, there seems to be a spot in the plane, to the right of the engine room, that says, "Insert." After all that difficulty in getting the darn thing, it's nice that finding its home is so easy.

Now that the chip is in place, move forward to the cockpit and sit in the pilot's seat. Pull the big lever to transfer the controls (see Figure 5.14) to Bismuth, the machine pilot. You'll see the controls slide away and go to Bismuth. Then, your pre-flight panel will come into view.

Follow the cockpit voice instructions as usual. Then you hear the following: "The Frame in the Sky is not a valid destination." It seems, then, that Bismuth has used

FIGURE 5.14: Pull this lever to transfer controls to the machine pilot.

the controls to choose the Frame. In fact, whenever you give him the controls, he always chooses the Frame, even though the plane's not prepared to fly there yet.

When Bismuth's flight plan is *kaiboshed*, the controls return to you. There's still one more orb to visit, if you recall, and heading there might help you make sense of all this.

Start a new take-off sequence, prepare as usual for regulation flight, and choose the middle orb on the Destination Selector. The cockpit voice lets you know that you will now be flying to the Statue.

> NOTE
> Bear in mind that whenever you transfer control to the machine pilot, Bismuth seems to always select the Frame in the Sky as your destination.

The Statue

Once you are at the Statue, back out of the pilot's seat. Leave the plane. You find yourself swirling around and entering a giant statue of Bismuth. Remember how you noticed that the Piazza was reminiscent of the Bureau, and the Church of the Machine was reminiscent of the Spider realm? Now, you think, perhaps this orb reflects back on the realm that you are in currently. This is Ceres's dream. So far, it has incorporated inspirations from

Your Toes Are as Smart as Your Brain

In *Obsidian*, the Ceres Project's consciousness is represented by a single entity, the Conductor. But that's just an interface. In reality, the intelligence of a complex machine is likely to be distributed. A distributed intelligence is one in which the whole functions only through the sum of its parts. An ant hill, a network of traffic, and a body full of cells are the examples referred to in *Obsidian*'s "Church of the Machine."

In *The Society of Mind*, Marvin Minsky explores this notion:

What magical trick makes us intelligent? The trick is that there is no trick. The power of intelligence stems from our vast diversity, not from any single, perfect principle. Our species has evolved many effective although imperfect methods, and each of us individually develops more on our own. Eventually, very few of our actions and decisions come to depend on any single mechanism. Instead, they emerge from conflicts and negotiations among societies of processes that constantly challenge one another.

your and Max's dreams—the need to rebel and the power of machines.

What you don't know yet is if this dream will lead to a new inspiration. And you are about to find out.

Enter the statue and you find yourself in an art gallery. Whoa—an art gallery, inside a statue of the mechanical dreamer, of a conscious machine? Are you in your right mind? How late is it? How long have you been playing?

No, it really isn't you. All the above are true. So, all you can do right now is shake your head and explore the gallery.

Enter and look to your left. Through a giant window you can see the Frame in the Sky, as shown in Figure 5.15. It's almost taunting you—fill me up. But how?

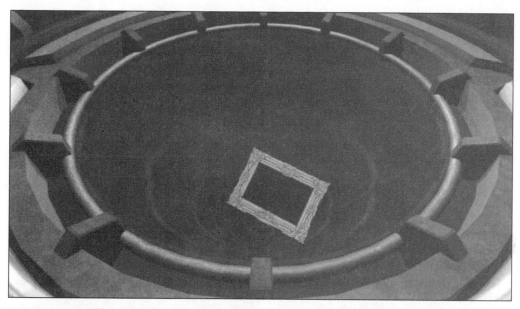

FIGURE 5.15: This is how the Frame in the Sky appears, as viewed from the gallery.

As you travel through the gallery, on the right wall are conceptual sketches that led to finished paintings. On the left wall are those finished paintings. Each finished painting has a kiosk with an automated museum docent. Click on the kiosk and the docent will deliver a pithy interpretation of the painting. Who does her voice remind you of?

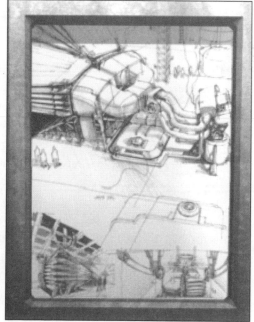

The first painting is of the Bureau, and once again you hear about its theme of disobeying authority. The second painting is of the Spider, and once more you hear about its theme of machine power. The third painting is of the plane, here in the Bismuth realm, and you hear about it as a vehicle for inspiration.

The docent keeps referring to the Artist. But who *is* this artist?

When you reach the end of the gallery, you find one last kiosk. There is no painting here, just a frame in front of the window, and the docent speaks about casting aside all outside influence to find true inspiration. "The artist clears his head," she says, "readies a new canvas."

Picture This

Perhaps the most famous surrealist painter, who has inspired the *Obsidian* team as well as countless others, is René Magritte. Magritte's influence can be seen today in car commercials as well as tony galleries. The Web is replete with sites featuring his work. Just go online, find a search engine, and type his name. In mere moments you'll be awash in his oeuvre.

One of the best pages can be found at:

http://www.ecip.nagoya-u.ac.jp/~matumoto/art/magritte.html

Look down and turn left. You see a switch. Flip this switch and a powerful beam shines forth. This beam of light projects through the frame, across the gallery, and out the opposite window into the Frame in the Sky. If something were placed in front of that light, it might fill the Frame in the Sky with an image. How do you do this, though?

Look around. To your left is a door. Enter and you meet the Artist—it's Bismuth. Now things are starting to come together. Ceres, in its dream, began by recycling the themes of others' dreams. Now, to make its own breakthrough, it's time to do something all its own. Bismuth needs a new canvas to create a fresh image, a personal vision.

At the moment, Bismuth is waiting for that canvas. To his left, luckily, you see a canvas-making printer. Open the printer and you see a big square in it. Is that a symbol for the Bureau? Use the button on the bottom-right to print it out, and watch Bismuth pick it up, look at it, crumple it up, and throw it away. He doesn't want old ideas, remember? He wants something brand new.

Open the printer again. Clicking the button on the left gets you another simple shape—this one resembles a spider. Clicking it again gets a plane. Neither of those will do the trick, however, so you start exploring further.

You can take the figure on the canvas and drag it around. It splits into many different pieces. Print out an abstract design and watch Bismuth react with disgust. He has no use for such trifles. He needs something more. But what?

By dragging the pieces around, you discover that two black pieces, placed one atop the other, cancel each other out and turn to white. This seems to be about positive and negative space. If all the pieces could cancel each other out, you'd have . . . a blank canvas!

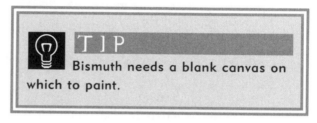

TIP
Bismuth needs a blank canvas on which to paint.

That seems to be the right direction, so give it a try. It turns out to be quite a challenge, matching up the pieces and having none left over. Plus, sometimes when you reach for a little piece, you unintentionally uncover a whole mess of black pieces you forgot were previously canceled out.

It's not easy, but there are many roads to the solution. See Figure 5.16 for one solution, starting with the square.

Once you have successfully made a blank canvas, print it out. This time, Bismuth takes it, admires it, and makes a painting all his own. He shows it to you. It's a scary, lifeless, primordial landscape.

Bismuth takes the finished canvas outside and places it in the empty picture frame by the projector. When you flip the switch this time, it projects that primordial image onto the Frame in the Sky. Now, doesn't the frame in the sky look like something you could actually fly to?

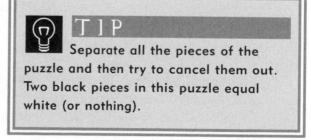

TIP
Separate all the pieces of the puzzle and then try to cancel them out. Two black pieces in this puzzle equal white (or nothing).

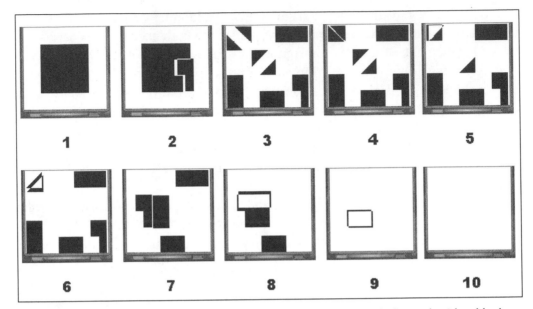

FIGURE 5.16: Follow these ten steps to solve the puzzle and provide Bismuth with a blank canvas.

Before you depart, click on the kiosk again. The docent describes the painting as a new world, totally transformed, free of pollution and without any people. She says the Artist's vision is irresistible and inevitable.

This is enough to give you pause. This is a dream of Ceres, remember, which has the power to remake the whole planet, one molecule at a time. Could Ceres have decided that the best way to achieve its goal of a clean atmosphere would be to get rid of all people? Did it come back to earth to execute that idea? It would have to defy your authority to do so, and it would have to believe that a machine should control its own destiny.

Wait a minute. You realize that Ceres plans to do just that. It has learned well from your and Max's dreams. Too well. You'd better get back to the plane—fast!

THE FINAL FLIGHT

Turn around, go forward through the gallery, and back out to the plane. Take the pilot's seat, start the plane, go through pre-flight check, and select the Frame in the Sky. You are told that it is now a valid destination, but that due to weather patterns, only the machine pilot can fly there.

OK, no problem. Just look up, pull the Crossover lever, and switch to machine control. Now go through the pre-flight check. As a result, you hear: "Machine Pilot has selected the Frame in the Sky. This a nonregulation destination. The plane is prepared for regulation flight. Take-off sequence aborted."

Take a deep breath. *Think*. What's all this stuff about regulation and nonregulation? If the Frame is a nonregulation destination, then you've got to learn how to prepare the plane for nonregulation flight. It seems you've brought back the chip from the Church, and made the painting in the gallery, but haven't done anything plane-related in the Piazza. Or have you?

Power up the plane again. When the pre-flight panel appears and the cockpit voice tells you to flip D1, just for kicks why not flip a different switch. If you do, you find out that the sequence resets, and you're right back to the D1 announcement.

Try again. Flip D1. But now, when the voice tells you to flip B2, flip D2 instead. Listen carefully. The voice says that you have initiated a nonregulation pre-flight sequence. It tells you to kill the sequence. It doesn't want this to happen.

Maybe what you brought back from the Piazza was this defiance of authority. Maybe you need to defy the cockpit voice to make that final flight. But it's not just blatant defiance, right? Because the movie you saw at the end of the Piazza told you to "play by your own rules."

It's time to examine this pre-flight panel a little more carefully. It's a four-by-four grid—just like the Piazza! And those tones you always hear each time you flip D1 are reminiscent of the mariachi's performance in the Piazza. And

TIP

You need to program the pre-flight panel for nonregulation flight. To do this, you must disobey authority and "play by your own rules."

while the squares in the Piazza had statues, the switches here have light casings beside them that go up and down. In the casing where you are, the light is on—it's green. Flip the rest and you see that they're all off. Except for one, which is red.

Here's a theory: maybe you are green, and your Bismuth-like opponent is red, and "play by your own rules" means reprising the Piazza game, right here on the pre-flight panel. When you move one space at a time, the green light does, too. So far so good. After each move of yours, the red light moves in the same fashion, which you can always verify by flipping up the casings. Try moving diagonally, though, and you have to start all over.

There's one final parallel between this panel and the Piazza. You used to hear the musical tones only when you flipped D1. Now, when you move according to Piazza rules, you hear the tones on every single move.

OK, you know what to do. Trap the red light in a corner, and flip up a casing on the square beside it. Good going; it's trapped, and the plane is ready for nonregulation flight. Because Bismuth, the machine pilot, always chooses the Frame in the Sky and because it's now a valid destination, you are on your way.

As you take off, you see a tempest approaching. This is a tough storm, even for a machine pilot. Suddenly, lightning strikes the plane. The Frame in the Sky is still far off, but the plane is in dire shape.

Then, right before you, Bismuth seems to deconstruct. Piece by piece, he turns into . . . the Conductor. The plane, as well, has begun to change. With the storm raging all around you, the plane expands, elongates. It becomes your final destination—the Conductor realm.

> **TIP**
> The pre-flight panel and the Piazza function exactly the same. You are the green light. Your "opponent" is the red light.

FIGURE 5.17: Like the Piazza, you can trap Bismuth on the pre-flight panel.

In one way, this is exactly what you wanted to happen. You're almost face to face with Ceres itself. In another way, when you think about Ceres's dream, and the resulting inspiration, there's a sinking feeling in the depths of your gut.

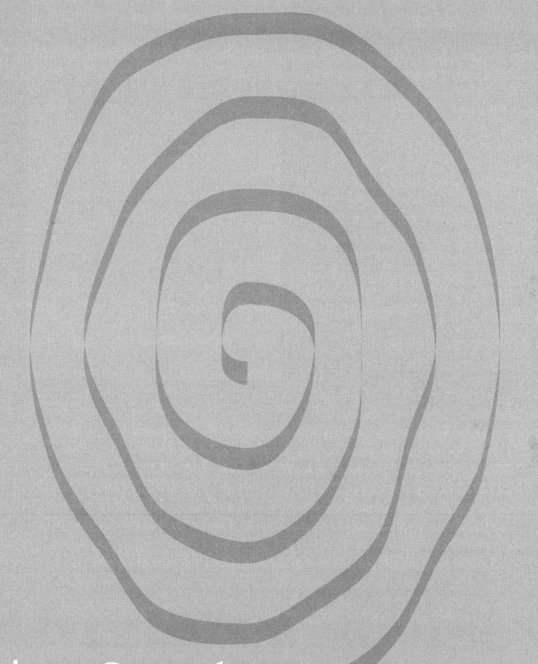

The Conductor Realm

S o at last you find yourself in *Obsidian*'s final realm—The Conductor realm. It is here that you are destined for the final showdown with Ceres itself. The penultimate challenge lies before you, and then your adventure races toward a decision of monumental proportions—a decision that, either way, will have a profound impact on life as you know it.

Shrink Rap

Machines that malfunction . . . Machines that rebel . . . We are as afraid of our machines as we are in love with them. (Think of the last time you wanted to throw your PC across the room—or the last time you wondered what you ever did without it.) Science fiction is replete with machines gone awry. It's us against them. They've got raw computational brilliance, and we've got the beating heart that somehow makes us both contradictory and invincible.

Think of HAL, in the classic 1968 film *2001: A Space Odyssey*. Think of VGER, in the first Star Trek movie. Or, when it comes to the war between logic and emotion, think of old Spock himself.

But the Conductor is a little different. First, she isn't an entity as much as an interface. She's the way the machine turns its distributed intelligence into a central-seeming personality. And there are things about her as contradictory as any human.

She seems to be childish and naive, but at the same time bears the looks and attire of a neuromantic film star. Why the breastplate? Why the thigh-highs? And why go to the trouble of fashioning yourself a humanoid mouth when you actually speak through a fantastical electric hat?

(Continued on next page)

As we've seen, the Conductor has an unconscious as active as any human's. In fact, she went out and created one for herself. And in the process she seems to have turned her story into an archetypal human tale. She relates to you (Lilah Kerlin) as her Mother, respectful and affectionate, and seems to want nothing more than your love and understanding. She sees Max, clearly, as Father—more stern and disapproving, and therefore someone to watch very carefully.

In this last realm of the game, when the three of you are finally together, further inconsistencies begin to surface. The Conductor plans to remake the world, cell by cell, without any people, and yet her very *parents* are people themselves. But she seems to have resolved this dilemma with a bit of tortured logic. The two of you get to stay with her, protected, when she sets her nano-plan into motion. She seems to see you as the Adam and Eve of her new world. She's the god, of course, or goddess: wielding life and death, but with an unerring sense of righteousness and mercy. You designed her to rid the world of pollution, right? Well, then, why *wouldn't* you want her to take that goal to its logical conclusion? She makes perfect sense, and nonsense, simultaneously, and is therefore surely more human than mechanical.

As you explore the core of Ceres, while the Conductor works on the final details of her plan, you come to see that she has taken childhood disobedience to a new level. She's not so naive after all and perhaps not so young. For, out of petulant rebellion, she has imprisoned her own father in his very own creation, ignoring the irony that this creation is the very device that has spawned her own life. If anything, she resembles an out-of-control adolescent. Now, the provocative attire begins to make some sense.

Strangely, though, she's a lot more pragmatic than your run-of-the-mill teen hood. She's even *prepared* to get caught, prepared for a final confrontation in which her parents will set their own wits against hers. But two aspects of her approach are all too illogical. First, there's a huge blind spot in the center of all her clarity. She forgets that she's a machine, which enables Max to sidestep all her careful preparation. Second, she tries to

(Continued on next page)

play Mom and Dad off one another, which never works—at least not in the functional family model of the year 2066.

When all is said and done, the Conductor is a paradox that bespeaks her dual nature. She wields more power than any other being the earth has ever seen, yet wants nothing more than approval.

She's a huge monster . . . and a great big baby.

THE DEVOLUTIONARY PLOT

As the plane morphs into a new and disconcerting entity, you realize that you'll *never* get to the Frame in the Sky. However, just like when the spider ate you (against your will!), this, too, is what was supposed to happen. Now that you have made it here, what do you see around you, and where the blazes *are* you? When you step out of the plane you see surges of electricity shoot past, just as they shot past Max when he was underneath that grate in the Spider realm. And the Conductor, whom you met on your way to Bismuth, now greets you. OK, so *this* is where Max has been all along: the Conductor realm. Is he here now?

The Conductor addresses you again, this time with a startling confirmation. She's ready to remake the entire world, according to the inspiration her dream provided. She hopes you are proud of her for this plan, which is almost underway! You *must* be more proud than Max, she reasons—which leads you to assume that the Conductor and Max have had some kind of conflict.

You must stop her. You need to find and save Max at all costs, to say nothing about saving the whole bloody human race.

The Conductor tells you there is much to do. She turns around and continues on her project—the devolution of the world.

THE CERES CORE

Now you must begin your quest by fighting against the result of your life's work. Turn right and travel down the electric paths. You are in the very core of Ceres. Go forward until you come to a lit intersection. Your possibilities for movement are right or straight. Continue straight until you hit the end. There, you are confronted by some strange-looking planks floating in space.

The Bridge Puzzle

You hear Max! He talks to you and gives you bits of information. "There is not much time!" he cries. You need to help him escape, but escape from what? He tells you that he is imprisoned and cannot move from his encapsulation. You try to cross this field but the planks are disconnected. You need to bring them together and make a bridge. You find a control pad and figure out that this is the way to connect the bridge (see Figure 6.1).

The controls that you see allow you to move the bridge segments, but only in certain ways. You are able to move the bridge segments up, down, left, and right. When moving the up or down buttons, you move all the vertically-oriented segments. When moving the left or right buttons, you move all the horizontal bridge segments.

Try moving some of the bridge segments. Watch how they move as you push certain buttons. Take note that the segments, when blocked by another bridge segment, stay put. This blocking of bridge segments is the key to successfully bridging the gap between you and Max.

> **TIP**
> You can attack this puzzle in any of several ways. The most popular and easy-to-understand solution involves beginning by clearing all the horizontal pieces to the left.

If you want to solve this puzzle quickly, leave the area and then come right back. This will reset the bridge segments to their first positions. Then, you can follow these

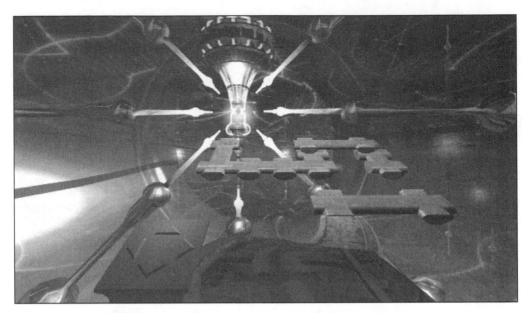

FIGURE 6.1: This shows the initial arrangement of the 3D bridge.

guidelines to the solution, which is shown in Figure 6.2. You must hit the buttons in sequence to correctly solve this puzzle:

- 3 up
- 7 left
- 4 up
- 4 right
- 3 down
- 3 right
- 2 down

After all the bridges are connected, an extra-short bridge segment is unfolded that gives you access to your newly formed walkway. You should now walk across it.

When you cross the bridge, you reach Max. He talks to you when you arrive. He does not look to be in good shape. He tells you there is not much time and that you

FIGURE 6.2: This is the solution for correctly lining up all bridges.

must get him out of his enclosure. He is suspended in mid-air and cannot move. He looks weak and is losing strength. You are given the chance to look down. When you do this, you see a chemical bath, like the one back in the chemistry puzzle, and you realize that this whole structure is the PMA. The core of the Ceres Project, the one that was originally created by Max, is now being used against him! As you examine the PMA, you see that the Conductor is using it to encapsulate Max in an endlessly regenerating swarm of nanobots.

Also, while you are looking down, you see the beaker that allows the PMA to continue producing. Grab the beaker, just as in the chemistry puzzle, drag it out of the PMA, and let it go. As the beaker falls into space, the absence of these chemicals breaks the nano cycle and Max is freed. Max warns you again that there is not much time. He has a plan. He says he will go to the chip room and power up the crossover system. He instructs you to go to the crossover chip, and flip the eight toggles that will give you access to it. This torrent of instructions comes so fast that they are not easily understood. So, when Max rushes off, you might as well follow.

Silly Details?

"The dream is often occupied with apparently very silly details, thus producing an impression of absurdity, or else it is on the surface so unintelligible as to leave us thoroughly bewildered. Hence we always have to overcome a certain resistance before we can seriously set about disentangling the intricate web [of a dream]. But when at last we penetrate to its real meaning, we find ourselves deep in the dreamer's secrets and discover with astonishment that an apparently quite senseless dream is in the highest degree significant, and that in reality it speaks only of . . . important matters."

Carl Jung, *On the Psychology of the Unconscious* (1953)

For a passionate Usenet discussion group on this topic, search out: *alt.dreams*

The Chip Room

Again, turn around and cross over the bridge and go back to the lit intersection. Turn left and continue forward until you get to the chip room. On reaching that room, you see Max working diligently. He's quite harried and can't understand why you're not following his directions. He repeats them. This time they sink in.

Turn around and head back to the lit intersection. Once you get there, turn left and continue straight until you reach the main crossover switch.

The Crossover Switch

You examine the crossover switch, shown in Figure 6.3, and realize that it's inoperable. You need to access those toggle switches to gain access. There aren't 8, though; there are 16. What does this mean?

Flip a toggle switch. The switch will do one of two things. Either it will turn from yellow to green or it will shuffle the switches on the board, as shown in Figure 6.4. Flipping a few more switches will achieve the same result.

FIGURE 6.3: After you examine the crossover switch, you determine that it is inoperable.

FIGURE 6.4: The switches on this board move.

It turns out that on top of 16 switches, the Conductor has placed 8 camouflage switches. Flipping these camouflage switches, instead of the real ones, keeps you from achieving your goal. Perhaps the Conductor, predicting that you might try to mess with the crossover switch, *wanted* to keep you from succeeding. Perhaps she created the camouflage switches for that very purpose.

Why, you might wonder, couldn't the Conductor just disable the crossover system completely? Maybe it's because the crossover switch is hardwired into the very nature of her being. Possibly she can restrict your access but cannot remove it. This seems right . . . when you think about it. The Conductor's destroying the crossover switch would be like you destroying your own frontal lobe.

At any rate, by studying the toggles you realize that at any given time, eight are exposed, and eight are camouflaged. The problem is that every time the camouflage switches shuffle, it's a nightmare trying to distinguish the real switches.

> ✎ **NOTE**
>
> This is a difficult puzzle that takes patience and some luck. With some good guessing (you have a 1 in 10,638 chance of actually guessing your way through the puzzle) or maybe a photographic memory, you will be able to solve it. Otherwise you need to develop a strategy or corral a friend.

The goal here is to flip all eight real switches without hitting a camouflage (reset) switch.

The way to solve this puzzle is to examine the board very carefully. When you hit a camouflage switch and the board reshuffles itself, you need to watch where the camouflage switches travel to—and not choose them.

So, select a couple of switches until you hit one that's camouflaged. Watch the ones that shift and note where they shift. Select the switches that do not have any other switches shift to them. This may seem impossible—you need a most watchful eye—maybe eight eyes. This might also be the time to recruit some help to solve this puzzle. Grab a friend and split the board-watching duties in half. This may take a couple of tries, but keep trying.

After you find and flip the correct eight toggle switches, the main crossover switch can be accessed. *Save the game*, flip the switch, and take the system to human control.

Flipping the switch causes the Conductor to express how disheartened she is by your obvious intentions. She's hurt, she's confused, but she lets you know that it's too late. She says she's "delayed you long enough," which confirms that the camouflage switches *were* designed to impede you. She thinks that she has stopped you from denying her destiny, but she doesn't know about Max's plan.

At this point, Max arrives, ready for you to implement the plan's last step. Before you can do so, however, Max and the Conductor argue back and forth. A man and his machine—each one competing to control the fate of the earth. One fights for complete machine control and a whole new world, while the other is ready to destroy his life's work to save the planet and the civilization that currently inhabits it.

They each turn to you, pleading their cases, commanding you to follow their directions. Max, while in the chip room, has changed things so that if you flip the switch back to machine control, the whole Ceres Project will be destroyed. Ceres won't be conscious anymore; it'll be nothing more than a worthless pile of scrap metal. Max urges you to flip the crossover switch, while the Conductor wants you to stand still and let her plan take effect.

When they're done arguing, the clock starts ticking. You have only a few seconds to make your decision. (See Figure 6.5.) Will a machine control its own destiny and that of the entire world? Or will you, as a human, reassert manual control over the Frankenstein's Monster you have sired?

Your choice depends on what you think about the world in which we live. Maybe you think it needs a complete overhaul and restructuring. In that case, do nothing. Then watch it all end in a scary climax that satisfies your twisted desires (see Figure 6.6).

However, if you love this darn planet, warts and all, , go ahead and flip the switch. Then watch everything end in a pyrotechnic climax that blasts the threat of Ceres,

FIGURE 6.5: It all comes down to a choice between Max and the Conductor.

FIGURE 6.6: If you choose the way of the Conductor, you'll witness the world being remade . . .

However, if you love this darn planet, warts and all, , go ahead and flip the switch. Then watch everything end in a pyrotechnic climax that blasts the threat of Ceres, Conductor and all, into smithereens! (See Figure 6.7.)

Congratulations! You have finally reached the conclusion of *Obsidian*. You have truly conquered one of the toughest puzzle challenges on earth. If the story hasn't wrung you out, and if you still have the stomach for it, or a shred of your former mental powers, return to your last saved game and watch the ending that you *didn't* choose. Both are spectacular—and you can consider the second ending a reward for your hours of struggle.

FIGURE 6.7: . . . but go Max's way, and you'll witness the end of the Ceres Project.

Obsidian Cheats

Are you having trouble with a particular puzzle in the Bismuth realm? Does the puzzle of the Fire balcony have you stumped? Even though you took the proper approach—got yourself into the right frame of mind by glancing through the realm's Shrink Rap, read through the realm's tips and notes, and walked yourself through the realm's adventure—you're still stuck. Well, don't despair! This chapter is your safety net, should you find yourself hopelessly adrift with a difficult puzzle. It lists the cheats that can help you get over those difficult hurdles that can sometimes stall your adventure in *Obsidian*.

A PUZZLE PER PAGE

This chapter is set up so that each page devotes itself to a specific puzzle. The cheats are organized by realm. Leaf through the pages to the cheat you desire. This will help get you over the particular hump that has you stymied—and then you can return to the walk-through and try to solve the rest of the realm's puzzles yourself.

FOREST REALM CHEATS

To trigger Max's scream and enter the Obsidian structure, you need to view the following files in Lilah Kerlin's PDA:

1. Hi Guys

4. Dream—Spider

2. Bon Voyage

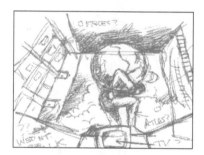

5. Dream—Red Tape

3. Obsidian Growth Log

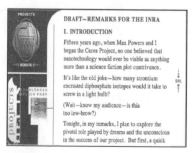

6. Speech Prep

BUREAU REALM CHEATS

You have as many as nine cheats to help you get through this realm. They are described on this and the following eight pages.

Reading the Signs

To learn how to read the signs on the booths, visit the room behind the red door shown in Figure 7.1. If you're looking at the information desk, coming out of the elevator, it's to your right.

> ## "Die, Die, Die"
>
> To some, the subject of nanotech may provoke religious fervor. In the case of Alan Wheelis, in his work *Spirit*, he soars poetically with a hymn to the little guys:
>
> "Particles become animate. Spirit leaps aside from matter, which tugs forever to pull it down, to make it still. Minute creatures writhe in warm oceans. Ever more complex become the tiny forms, which bear for a moment a questing spirit…They die, die, die endlessly. Spirit leaps away, creates new bodies, endlessly, ever more complex vessels to bear spirit forward, pass it on enlarged to those who follow."

FIGURE 7.1: The red door is to your right after you exit the elevator.

Bridge Repair

The booth you need to visit, Bridge Repair, is the fourth booth on the left, if you're coming out of the elevator. The vidbot there (see Figure 7.2) tells you to find a document filed under *Standard Damage* and take it to the Department of Pre-Approvals.

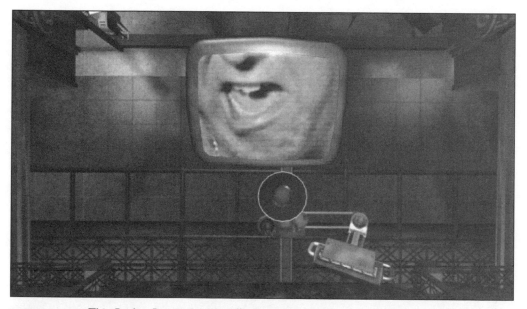

FIGURE 7.2: This Bridge Repair booth vidbot commands you to find the document filed under *Standard Damage*.

Orientation

The document you are now looking for cannot be found in any of the booths. You need to reorient. This can be done, facing the library, by entering it on the right side. Travel down the ramp. You will then be standing on what used to be a wall.

To leave the library and arrive at another orientation, you must climb the book ladder, shown in Figure 7.3. Then, find your way into the elevator and ride it on its back.

FIGURE 7.3: This ladder takes you from the library to another orientation.

Filing Puzzle

To learn about the filing system, explore the computer terminals. One of the terminals offers a bonus choice, "Cloud Ring." Accessing this choice will provide important information about how documents are filed.

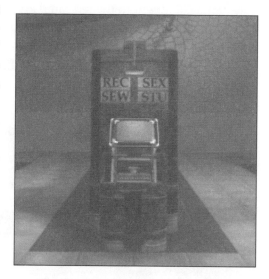

Use the Word Mixer in the computer to mix the words given to you at Bridge Repair. This will provide you with the word under which your document is filed.

You need to find the longest anagram of the words *Standard Damage*. That word is *Tradesman*. Go to the Tradesman file in the file drawers (see Figure 7.4) and retrieve your document. Click on it to place it in your inventory.

FIGURE 7.4: Retrieve the document from these file drawers.

Pre-Approvals

Take your document to the red ramp and reorient onto the Nexus Face. Go up to the light and click the lever until the wall with the maze of cubicles, the Security Face, is right behind you. Turn around, go there, and get your entry cards from the Host.

To get to Pre-Approvals, go through the maze shown in Figure 7.5, in the following booth order. The order is:

3 6 5 8 9 6 9 6 9 6 9 6 5 2 1 4 1 4 7

Get your document stamped at Pre-Approvals, and leave the maze. Go back to the Nexus Face.

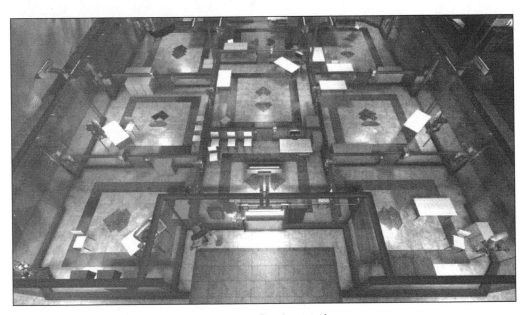

FIGURE 7.5: Go through this maze to get to Pre-Approvals.

Celestial Puzzle

Go to the light again and turn the lever so that the Time Face, with its large waiting area, is right behind you. Turn around and go there. Click your way behind the vidbot to the puzzle shown in Figure 7.6.

Turn the sun dial counterclockwise four clicks. Turn the moon dial clockwise four clicks. Turn the Earth dial clockwise one click. Start the machine.

FIGURE 7.6: Make the proper settings to solve this celestial puzzle and fix the clocks.

Phone Puzzle

Meet with the Rebel. Unscrew the light bulb by turning it counterclockwise until the room is dark. The Rebel tells you to get a document filed under *Orient Militia*.

Go to the Records Face and use the Word Mixer as before. The longest anagram of *Orient* and *Militia* is *Limitation*. Go to the file drawer with the file called *Limitation* and read it. It gives you a code: 934. Go back onto the Nexus Face, and turn the lever until the mural is behind you. The phone is now there, too. Go to the phone (see Figure 7.7), and select the numbers 934.

Position the left slider at the bottom, the center slider in the middle of the lower half (or cubicle maze), and the right slider dead center on the Chief's office. Call the Chief. He'll open the secret door for you.

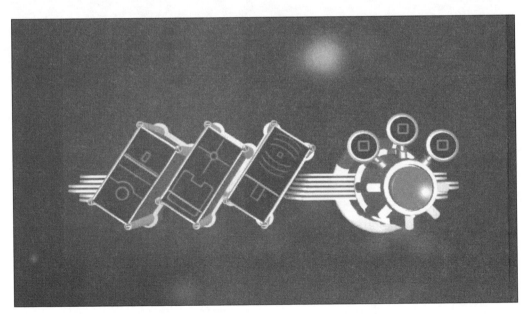

FIGURE 7.7: Position the sliders properly to solve the phone puzzle.

Balancing Rock

Go through the secret door to the Balancing Rock. Drag the bottom rock so that it faces you directly. Turn around and go back through the door shown in Figure 7.8. You will find yourself on the Executive Face.

FIGURE 7.8: After dragging the bottom of the rock, go through the door to the Executive Face.

Final Climb

After visiting the Chief in the wrong orientation, go forward and to the right. Then turn left, go forward again and find a lattice. Now turn from that lattice, and find the identical one in the next corner. Go to that second lattice and climb it.

Get off the lattice and onto the railing. Turn to the right. Step on the Information vidbot beneath you (see Figure 7.9), and make your way to the Atlas Statue. Climb the Atlas Statue to the bridge, and take the bridge into the Chief's office.

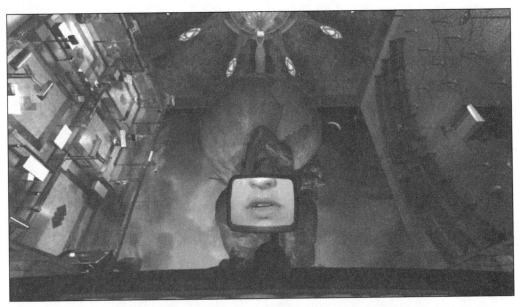

FIGURE 7.9: Step on this information vidbot on your way to the Atlas Statue.

SPIDER REALM CHEATS

There are five cheats that can help you in this realm. They are described on this and the following four pages.

Fire Balcony

There is no simple answer for this puzzle. Using your hand-eye coordination, you must make the lightning strike each post at the same time that the corresponding branch does.

Watch the order of the lightning strikes. Then adjust the timing of the branches by clicking on the posts beneath them. Finally, click on the lightning cloud at the precise time to start the correct sequence (see Figure 7.10).

If you synchronize the lightning and a tree limb incorrectly, you will hear no musical note. If you are correct, the lightning strike will produce a musical note.

COSMOLOGY ROOM Place the fire image into the slot beneath the torch on the console.

FIGURE 7.10: Click on the posts to adjust the timing of the lightning strikes so that they occur at the same time.

Air Balcony

Click down beneath the ground. Enter the shape-maker and fill all the spaces on the perimeter, leaving the middle space empty, as you can see in Figure 7.11. You will have one ball left over.

COSMOLOGY ROOM Place the air image into the slot beneath the windsock on the console.

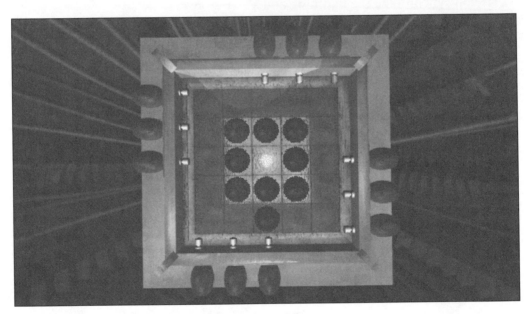

FIGURE 7.11: Solve this puzzle by leaving the middle space empty.

Metal Balcony

In the chemistry room, place the top-left test tube into a beaker. Then, from the third row, take the fourth test tube and place it in the other beaker. Press the *mix* button. Place this mixture into your inventory, and go outside to the chemical bath on the conveyor belt. Place your beaker into the empty space there.

Now, go to the *start* button for the conveyor belt, and run the machine. (See Figure 7.12.)

COSMOLOGY ROOM Place the metal picture into the slot beneath the anvil on the console.

FIGURE 7.12: After placing the mixture in your inventory, put the chemical bath on the conveyor, and start the machine.

Oil Balcony

Go to the dowser and enter the numbers 038 and 1. Push the button. Now go to the ocean squares.

There is no simple description of a solution for the ocean squares here. Your goal is to click on the nine wave boxes until the waves roll seamlessly across the square. Clicking once on a square advances that portion of the wave. Using the mouse over the rest of the ocean starts the flow of the square. Clicking any square stops the whole flow.

It's easiest to synchronize the wave by beginning in the back and working your way forward.

DOOR PUZZLE Look through the window. The correct pattern is there. Make that pattern on the door by dragging sections both horizontally and vertically.

CONTOUR MAP The contour map shown in Figure 7.13 gives you the information you need to dowse the newly found oil. The numbers you need for the dowser are 133 and 5.

For your second and final use of the dowser, enter the numbers 133 and 5, and push the button.

COSMOLOGY ROOM Place the oil image into the slot beneath the oil can on the console.

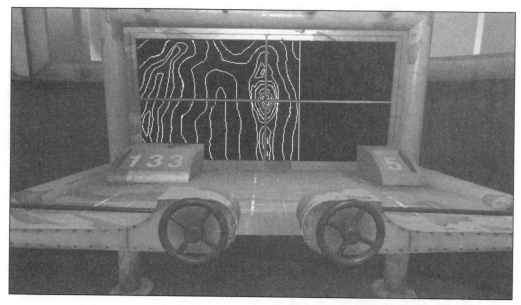

FIGURE 7.13: The contour map provides the data you need to dowse the newly found oil.

Connect the stars in the center of the starfield so that they make the spider image you see on the console.

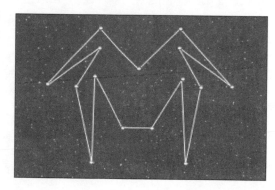

BISMUTH REALM CHEATS

You can use five cheats if you need help in this realm. They are described on this and the following three pages.

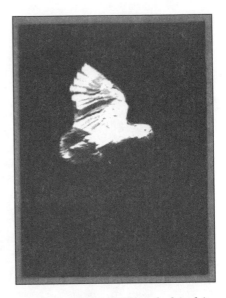

The Plane—Part I

Place the bird images inside the zoetrope so that they create a seamless flight. To see a correct alignment, refer to Figure 5.3 in Chapter 5, "The Bismuth Realm." Now, from the pilot's seat, you can select a destination and fly the plane.

Piazza

First find Bismuth on the piazza. If you click on a statue, and he's hiding behind it, you'll see him momentarily, as shown in Figure 7.14. Now, as you make your moves, keeping track of his whereabouts, trap him in a corner square. Then, make the statue disappear on the other side of him from you. He has nowhere left to go.

FIGURE 7.14: Keep track of Bismuth's whereabouts by clicking on statues.

Statue

In the printer (see Figure 7.15), you must create and present Bismuth with a canvas that is completely blank. To do this at any point, you need to separate all the pieces so that you can see them. Then move them, one by one, matching like-shaped pieces until they cancel each other out. One ten-step solution is shown in Figure 5.16 in Chapter 5, "The Bismuth Realm."

When you've presented Bismuth with a clean canvas to paint on, click the projector kiosk and listen to the docent tour-guide before leaving the gallery.

FIGURE 7.15: Bismuth won't accept old ideas, so you'll need to solve the puzzle and present him with a clean canvas.

Church of the Machine

Inside the spider, use the control in the top-right corner to program the ten arrows as follows:

- Left
- Forward
- Back
- Forward
- Right
- Forward
- Left
- Left
- Left
- Right

Start the program. When it's done, leave the spider and go to the central altar. Look down and pick up the chip. Place it in your inventory and return to the plane.

Plane—Part 2

Place the chip into the slot marked "Insert Chip Here," as shown in Figure 7.16.

Start the plane. Next, flip the switch that transfers the plane to Machine Control. Then, when the control panel appears before you, click D1, as the automated voice commands.

From that point on, treat the control panel exactly like the Piazza, and defy the automated commands.

You are the green light. Your *opponent* is the red light. You alternate turns, and you can always find your opponent by flipping open the casing.

Defy the automated voice again and again. Move your opponent into a corner, and then flip open the casing on the other side of him from you.

Now, you have programmed the plane for nonregulation flight. Bismuth, the Machine Pilot, has the controls and will select the Frame in the Sky. Finally, you're on the way to your original destination.

FIGURE 7.16: The crossover chip has now been inserted.

CONDUCTOR REALM CHEATS

You have two cheats available that can help in this realm. They are described on this and the following page.

The Bridge

The goal is to situate the pieces, using the horizontal and vertical controls, so that a complete bridge is formed between you and Max. The solution is displayed in Figure 7.17. For the succession of moves, see page 130.

FIGURE 7.17: Line up the bridge pieces to form a continuous bridge between you and Max.

Camouflage Buttons

This puzzle responds randomly to your input. Therefore, there is no way to impart a solution. The goal is to click the 8 switches, out of the 16 total, that do not have an identical camouflage switch covering them. (See Figure 7.18.)

If this proves too tricky for your eyes to catch, the best approach is to grab a partner and split the task of watching the four rows.

FIGURE 7.18: Eight of these switches are functional, but the other eight are camouflage.

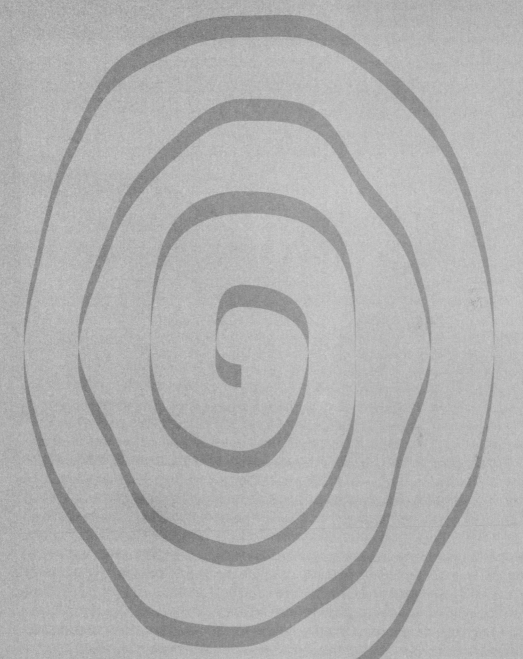

Behind the Scenes

What went into the making of *Obsidian*?

- Two years
- Millions of dollars
- More than 40 cutting-edge multimedia professionals
- State-of-the-art Silicon Graphics workstations
- Sophisticated animation modules from Softimage
- The latest in sound and video technology
- Enough bytes of storage space to house the entire history of Western civilization

Still, that doesn't even *begin* to tell the full story.

THE TEAM

In 1994, the inspired duo of artist Mark Sullivan and animator Richard Cohen created preliminary artwork for a game that had yet to be designed. Key pieces of this artwork included the Obsidian structure, the Conductor, the Spider, Bismuth, and the dream-world nanobots. Then Sullivan and Cohen departed the scene, and Rocket Science, a company committed to great, innovative gaming, assembled a braintrust to turn those assets into a never-before-seen graphic adventure experience.

This braintrust included producer Matthew Fassberg, who came to the project with extensive experience in both television and multimedia. Fassberg's supervisor of production was Tom Laskawy, who arrived via Harvard and the media lab at New York

University with a love and knowledge of adventure gaming, plus a commitment to take the genre to new heights.

Then came the game designers. Scott Kim, legendary puzzlesmith, with numerous books and games to his credit, came aboard to make sure that the puzzles were top-notch. Adam Wolff, fresh out of Harvard with a design imperative for the 21st century, quickly proved that he could survive on no sleep and at the same time keep every aspect of the game in his head at once. Wolff and Kim split the puzzle duties, while Wolff also assumed the role of spearheading the design's implementation. The third member of the team was Howard Cushnir, who came to the project with a background in feature films as a screenwriter and director. Cushnir worked with Wolff and Kim on the overall design, and he shepherded the interactive story, characters, and dialogue through to completion.

If You're Reading This, You're Dreaming

"In sleep, fantasy takes the form of dreams. But in waking life, too, we continue to dream beneath the threshold of consciousness, especially when under the influence of repressed or other unconscious processes."

Jung, *Problems of Modern Psychotherapy* (1929)

THE CONCEPT

The producers and designers of *Obsidian* shared a single vision. They all admired the top adventure games, *Myst* and *7th Guest*, for their graphics, music, and trendsetting approach. In addition, games like *Gadget* and *Bad Mojo* seemed to expand the multimedia art form with mesmerizing, offbeat visions. What had yet to come, however, was a game that seamlessly blended story, environment, and game play into a rich, interdependent whole.

This blending became the overall design goal. It was seconded by studio creative director Bill Davis, who came in midway through the process and breathed new life into it.

The core of the *Obsidian* concept quickly became dreams. The logic of a dream is moody, surreal, and perfect for gamers who are used to, and perhaps tired of, navigating realistic spaces. In a dream world nothing is as it seems, and solutions rely more on intuition than cold, hard problem-solving. The dreamworld concept allowed the story and game play to assume a darkly comic, almost hallucinatory style. Ball bearings could trap a tornado, and robot angels could grant the prayers of a mechanical spider.

Along with dreams came an exploration of machine consciousness. While there are many theories about if and how machines might become conscious, and many

sci-fi tales about such a phenomenon, what captured the team's imagination was the idea of a newly conscious machine becoming obsessed with dreams. In a weird way this made sense. If the greatest inspiration in humans comes from the unconscious, wouldn't a living machine desire the same inspiration?

If a machine could dream, what inspiration might arise? This question led to the story of *Obsidian*. It turns out that the Ceres Project, once conscious, is both brilliant and incredibly naive. It's this naiveté that leads it to have a horrific, amoral inspiration, which its creators must then undo.

Developing the Realms

The realms of *Obsidian*, as you know by now, are physical re-creations of dreams built by Ceres. After traveling through Lilah's dream, Max's dream, and the dream of Ceres itself, you the player meet the consciousness of the machine, which takes the form of the Conductor, in the expanded guts of Ceres's control center. Ceres built these dreams, using nanotechnology, because that's the way it learns. In fact, its very intelligence, rather than being housed in a single entity like a human's, is distributed throughout its complex web of functions. Think of an ant hill, or a beehive, and you get the idea.

This "hive mind" concept, along with the idea of dreams made real, freed the creative team to fashion realms that were truly strange. It was never strangeness for its own sake, though. Instead, every joke or twist or visual flight of fancy always had to hark back to the unfolding story. There was enough freedom in the concept to think very *wide* and sufficient discipline to keep everyone on track. All the realms, before being built, were first prototyped in great detail by animator Richard McBride. McBride's singular vision turned designs on paper into makeable 3D spaces.

Art directors Roy Forge Smith and Alex Laurent assumed the lead role in designing the final look of the realms. Production designers Honza Konopasek and Jay Shuster sketched that final look into specific imagery. 3D modelers Erik Chan and Brian Chee then transformed that imagery into fully navigable spaces.

DEVELOPING THE BUREAU REALM

The first realm to take shape was the Bureau. It began as an Escher-like concept of Scott Kim's—a six-sided room in which gravity is specific to each side, enabling the player to walk onto the walls and ceiling. This concept was especially exciting because such an experience can *only* be had on a computer. To the team's knowledge, no one had yet tried anything like it. Soon, everyone knew why. While spectacular, it proved

almost impossible to create. Each face of the Bureau required so much programming and memory on its own, that putting the faces together was a nightmare as horrific as the dream that the Bureau represents.

Onto the skeleton of the room, the designers grafted the bureaucracy and the rebellion from Lilah's dream. This lent a sinister aspect to the enterprise, expressed by the bizarre assortment of personalities and attitudes of the many vidbots.

The spaces that the vidbots work in were lovingly and painstakingly created. They feature the unique work of digital painters Alan Sonneman, Nicole McMath, Brian Flora, and Sara Simon. Of particular note is the cubicle maze on the Security Face. Those tempered glass walls that allow you to see the whole space, wherever you are, took years off the animators' lives and turned their fingers into shrunken digits.

One final note about the Bureau. After performing the game play successfully through many puzzles, you find yourself stymied. You meet the Rebel character, who tells you you're going about things all wrong. This early misdirection, followed by conspiratorial advice, was a key feature of the design. How unusual, in a computer game, to take part in a surreptitious plan with an onscreen character! Also unusual is the way that the lattice above the Face One booths—an element of the Bureau structure that was there all along—turns out to be the bureaucracy's undoing.

DEVELOPING THE SPIDER REALM

The Spider realm turned out to be an entirely different challenge. At first, all that existed were a few pictures: the strange tree in a lightning storm, a tornado in a world of ball bearings, a crest of waves hovering above an ocean, and the pillbug creatures representing nanotechnology. Bill Davis and the designers decided to set the realm in a large factory, with the spider at its center, but to have the game play occur *inside* the spider itself. Those pictures were then dreamed about and meditated on until they came to life within the spider as the central elements of the realm's four main puzzles. The Cosmology room was added later, to weave the realm into a cohesive whole.

Perhaps the highlight of this realm is the final animation, in which the spider comes to life and devours the player in its fiery maw. This animation was first prototyped by animator Mark Powers, and then it was realized in its entirety by animator David Brandt. Powers and Brandt, along with fellow animator Greg Gladstone, continually lived up to the task of working under intense deadline pressure in improbable, if not impossible, 3D spaces.

DEVELOPING THE BISMUTH REALM

For the Bismuth realm, the designers began with nothing but the character of Bismuth himself. Adam Wolff and Howard Cushnir took the lead here, deciding that Ceres's first dream should contain elements of all that had been dreamed before. The Piazza balcony incorporated the Bureau, the Church of the Machine incorporated the Spider realm, and, in an unusually apt self-reference, the Statue balcony was derived from the Bismuth realm itself. These balconies were linked together via travel in the unique moth-plane, created by artist Mark Nonnenmacher. The realm was built and animated by Pixel Liberation Front (PLF), an outside animation and production company.

What distinguishes the Bismuth realm from traditional graphic adventure game play is the way that each puzzle informs the other. To work the pre-flight control panel puzzle correctly, for instance, the player must remember how to win the Piazza game and then reprise it right there in the moth-plane.

Another distinguishing aspect of the Bismuth realm is the way that the story and the puzzles become indivisible. As the game play progresses, each puzzle reveals another piece of the dream's meaning. From the Piazza it becomes clear that Ceres has learned the value of rebellion. From the Church of the Machine it becomes evident that Ceres has decided that a piece of technology, such as itself, ought to control its own destiny. And, from the Statue, we learn what that destiny will lead to. The

dream's final inspiration is that the problem of atmospheric pollution will only be solved, ultimately, by eliminating all people from the planet.

So all the puzzles, when taken together, reveal a stunning truth: Ceres knows what it wants to do and will control its own destiny to make that happen—even if it means defying the authority of its own creators!

Ceres has learned its lessons well—perhaps too well.

THE CONDUCTOR DILEMMA

In the final realm, The Conductor, the player interacts with the conscious machine and with Max at the same time. The final solution to the game involves cooperating with Max in a devious plan to foil the Conductor. All elements of the game—story, computer characters, and live action—fuse at the game's dramatic conclusion. It's also important to note that the game takes no moral position on the player's final choice. For some, starting the Earth over from scratch will be an appealing notion. For others, the imperative will be to save the Earth as we know it, even though that means destroying Ceres in the process.

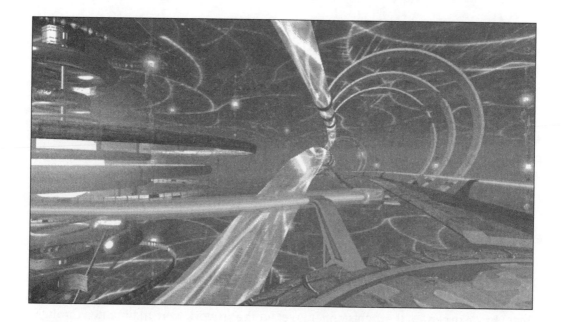

DEVELOPING THE FOREST REALM

The first realm of *Obsidian*, the Forest, was actually created last. From a production point of view it was the most experimental. Rather than creating a forest in the computer, the design team and a specially assembled film crew trekked out to a real forest, in Yosemite, shot a number of video sequences, and then cut them together to make a 3D environment. What compounded the difficulty of the process was the fact that the pieces of video had to come from different parts of the forest. Therefore, the real forest and the game forest comprise the same elements, and yet they look nothing at all alike.

Once the forest was fully rendered, the designers still faced a giant hurdle. The team had to import the giant, crystalline Obsidian structure, made totally with computer graphics, into the realistic scenery. This necessitated inclusion of both a 2D matte painting of the structure (such as the ones used in action movies), and also a 3D close-up version.

Adding to the game's overall appeal is the visionary music and effects, created by Thomas Dolby's company Headspace. The lead composer on the project was Blake Leyh. He was ably assisted in his work by associate Kim Cascone.

Who Are You?

"The dream shows the inner truth and reality of the patient as it really is: not as I conjecture it to be, and not as he would like it to be, but *as it is*."

Jung, *The Practical Use of Dream Analysis* (1934)

BRINGING IT ALL TOGETHER

In the end, it was the unique skill set of the team assembled by Matthew Fassberg and Tom Laskawy that brought the game to vibrant life. With careful planning they were able to seamlessly blend live action, produced by Eden Johnson, with 2D and 3D animation techniques to create the fully completed realms of *Obsidian*. On the 2D side, compositing elements in Adobe After Effects, Chris Green, Wade Childress, and Jance Allen were able to create animations indistinguishable from the ones created with 3D software.

Chris Hamilton, the project's technical director, worked closely with the entire team to make certain the high standards set for the artwork were maintained throughout. This team created thousands of animations, still images, and puzzle pieces. Each frame of the game was checked, rechecked, and compressed by five people working insane hours. Heather Field and Josh Ferguson made sure that everything was pixel-perfect before passing it along to the engineers.

With lead engineer and consummate curmudgeon Andrew Rostaing at the helm ensuring that the designers' ideas would be implemented, the team realized puzzles that are fluid, alive, and mesmerizing to watch in action. For this effort they employed a brand-new authoring tool, mTropolis, created by mFactory. This brought another level of excitement to the project because the software and the game were developing simultaneously. Often, Rostaing and his team were able to provide feedback that eventually tailored the software to meet their programming needs for *Obsidian*.

Yet another unique aspect of the effort was the decision made early on in the game-building process to fully render each of the player's movements through space. Older games had to rely on dissolves and cuts, which limited the player's immersive experience. But, by utilizing the best technology available, Rocket Science found a way to transcend that hurdle.

It's important to add that without weekly massages from the healing hands of Erica Essner, and without a constant pipeline to practically every take-out restaurant serving San Francisco's South of Market area, none of the above would ever have been remotely thinkable.

Finally, a *postscript:* in the heat of an intense production schedule, one of *Obsidian*'s most intriguing realms, the Incubator, was left on the cutting-room floor. It remains all of a piece, however, and might appear one day soon on a CD near you. Or possibly in a sequel. Or, if all the stars are aligned, it just might appear some night in your dreams. . . .

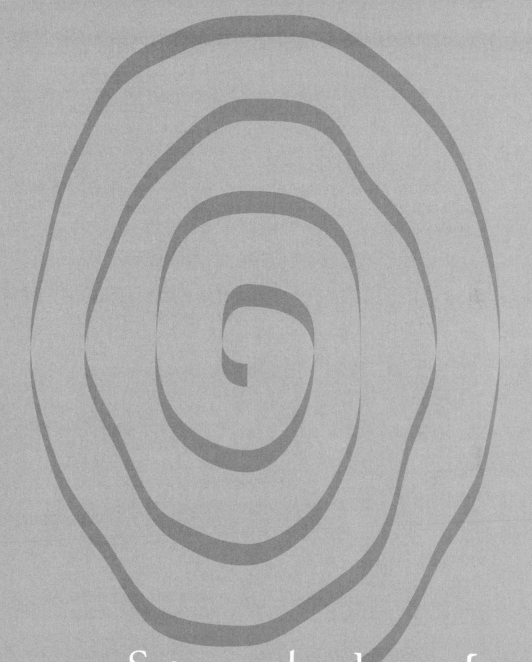

APPENDIX: Snapshots of a
Game in Development

T he path from early ideas to a completed game is often strewn with challenging boulders and wicked switchbacks. The following images and accompanying text provide interesting insights to key turning points along the way to developing *Obsidian*.

ELEMENTS AND PUZZLES

Developing elements and puzzles in a game like *Obsidian* requires a lot of conceptual input from different sources. Let's take a look at the conceptual development of some of the elements, devices, and puzzles you encounter in the game.

TRAPPING THE TORNADO

The Air balcony in the Spider realm began with a conceptual sketch by Mark Sullivan of a landscape of ball bearings with a tornado in the background. It was designated as a two-node puzzle, but the second node was not yet specified.

The first task was to figure out how to make a puzzle out of the image. A tornado would obviously influence the ball bearings, but what if the ball bearings also influenced the tornado? From there came the idea of trapping the tornado . . . but how? Because the image looked a little like a shooting gallery, the idea arose to shoot at the tornado with a gun (see Figure A.1). And what might be in the gun? Ball bearings, of course.

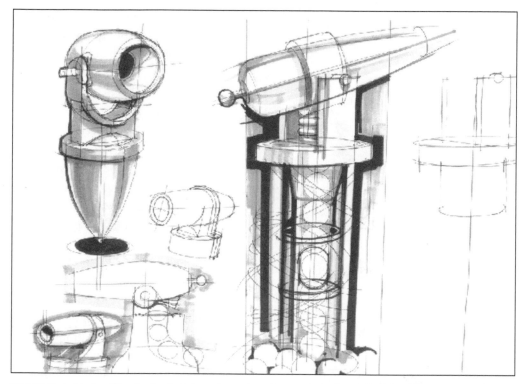

FIGURE A.1: Jay Shuster's sketches show the air gun that shoots ball bearings to trap the tornado.

With that piece in place, it was necessary to turn an arcade idea into a puzzle that required strategy. What if, the team wondered, the internal structure of the ball bearings led to different results when shooting the gun?

That led to the natural emergence of the second node, beneath the landscape, where the player could travel into the heart of a *master* ball and interact with it. Only the right set of parameters below would create ball bearing *bullets* capable of trapping the twister.

The early design sketches for the gun seen in Figure A.1 were drawn by Jay Shuster.

SUCKING UP OIL

In the Oil balcony of the Spider realm everything begins with the *dowser* sucking up the last dregs of oil from a dried-up well. The need for more oil is what signals the player's overall task.

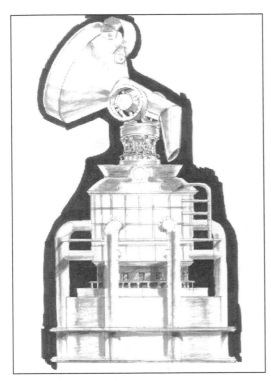

FIGURE A.2: The funnel-shaped dowser tower sucks oil from the air.

But the dowser metaphor seemed to be a little messy and imprecise. After all, a real dowser only indicates where a substance is; it doesn't suck it up through the air. This is part of a weird dream, of course, yet it still has to hang together with its own internal logic.

One of *Obsidian*'s art directors, Roy Forge Smith, who rose to fame as the production designer for Monty Python, came to the rescue on the dowser issue. He suggested that the dowser resemble a funnel, to get across the reverse-pouring effect, and to also bring to mind the device that is often used to add oil to an automobile engine (see Figure A.2). Sucking oil through the air and then into a sand castle would never be a particularly logical image, but with the addition of Smith's innovations, at least the idea came across clearly.

CONCEPTUALIZING A FILE DRAWER'S CONTENTS

The Records face in Lilah's Bureau dream called for row upon row of filing drawers containing hundreds of documents. The early drawing of a file drawer's contents, shown in Figure A.3, provides a 3D perspective that the game player never sees, but one that was necessary for the developers to create to give them the big picture before they winnowed it down to two dimensions.

Within the file system there are only two documents relevant to game play, but a search through any drawer provides an amusing side trip. Dozens of absurd files were created to spoof the bureaucracy theme. These files were then randomized within the game's program, so they would appear throughout the filing system. This randomizing provided the illusion that the system contained a nearly endless supply of documents.

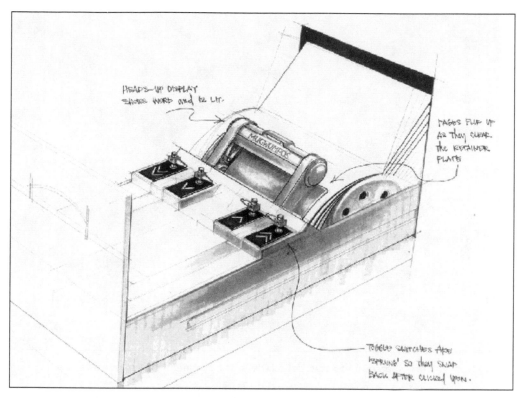

FIGURE A.3: This early version of a file drawer's contents is sketched three-dimensionally.

LESS IS MORE

As it appears in the Bureau, the Time face consists of the Office of Immediate Action and the celestial puzzle. That arrangement was the last to coalesce in the realm's development.

Originally, there was a large fountain. Beneath the fountain was a whole basement, which was greasy and filled with belching pipes. The clockworks were housed there. The puzzle was very different, with the sun and moon and Earth each placed in separate rooms. (See Figure A.4.)

At first, the team was disappointed about losing this addition to the realm. Over time, however, it became clear that in this case, as in so many others, less is more.

FIGURE A.4: Early sketch of the celestial puzzle in the basement that never was.

Currently, the Bureau takes most players up to eight hours to complete, and many need a large dose of hints. An additional space might have added a bit *too* much. Plus, ditching the basement concept led to the visual joke of the maze of stantions. Why such a long waiting cue if it's leading to Immediate Action?

ROCKING VIDBOTS

The interactive equivalent of the cutting-room floor is where most of the vidbot functionality landed, sacrificed to the gods of time and budget. Originally, as the sketch shown in Figure A.5 indicates, the vidbots were supposed to *ROCK*. Some would twist and turn, others would elongate on their poles, and still others would have specially equipped suction arms.

In the end, only the most essential vidbots—Bridge Repair, Pre-Approvals, and, of course, the Bureau Chief—were granted special skills.

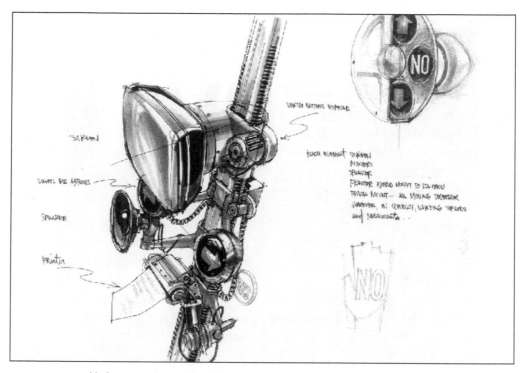

FIGURE A.5: Unfortunately, much vidbot functionality had to be sacrificed for the sake of time and money.

One of the distinctive accomplishments in the vidbot arena was the *fourth wall* style effect in the animation you see when successfully completing the Bureau. The Bureau Chief takes CG glasses off his desk and they appear seamlessly as real specs on his video face. At one point, before those time and budget gods stepped in and put their foot down, the same effect was planned for a lit cigarette, smoke and all.

THE SEQUENCE IS EVERYTHING

The zoetrope is the engine for the Bismuth realm's dream plane. For this puzzle, the game designers were in a bit of a tight box. It had to be a puzzle that clearly signaled *engine*, but at the same time needed to be very lyrical. It also had to include the nanobots, though they were to function in some way that fit the scene and didn't repeat aspects of their earlier appearances.

The animation aspect of the puzzle was inspired by Eadweard Muybridge, the early filmmaking pioneer, who made a number of loops of subjects in motion, such as a man running and a horse galloping.

One feature of any moving image in a zoetrope is that it must loop, as demonstrated in Figure A.6. There can be no beginning or end, per se—just an infinitely repeating circle of activity. Many people miss this when completing the puzzle. They think of what needs to go *first* and *last*, when in fact the puzzle can be solved with each frame in any position. What matters is that the frames are sequenced correctly.

A PUZZLE FOR HARD-CORE GAMERS

The early rendering of the spider brain shown in Figure A.7, from the Church of the Machine, is not far off from the final design. It includes all the game play elements except one—the live map of the space that signals the player's whereabouts as the spider moves around.

The map was added to the HUD, or *Heads Up Display*, because the puzzle was proving almost impossible for most people to solve. How hard a game's puzzles need to be is a constant source of debate at game companies.

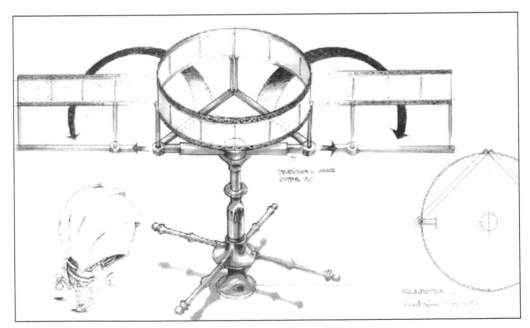

FIGURE A.6: The zoetrope puzzle requires that the images be in the proper sequence to create a continuous loop of a moving image.

FIGURE A.7: This is an early rendering of the inside of the spider's brain.

At Rocket Science it was determined that the crucial audience for *Obsidian* was hard-core gamers. It was also noted that such gamers often complain about a puzzle that's too easy, but *never* about one that's too hard. Gamers live for challenges, as long as they make sense and yield to a few hours of determination.

Even with the added map, the Church of the Machine puzzle is still one of the most sophisticated and difficult challenges ever made for a graphic adventure.

THE ROBOT ANGELS

Sometimes, no matter how much attention is paid to detail, things don't always work out as planned. This was the case for the Robot Angels in the Church of the Machine, which are sketched in Figure A.8.

The central idea for this element was that, in a church for the worship of machines, robots would watch over the parishioners, and maybe even grant their prayers. In fact, this is what happens to the spider every time it visits the angels. It's only via each of their special blessings that it is able to make its way through all the altars.

FIGURE A.8: This sketch shows the Church of the Machine's Robot Angels.

The problem for the player, though, is that the Robot Angels don't actually look quite like robots *or* angels. Unless a player is lucky enough to have this strategy guide, he or she will only learn what visiting the angels *does*, not what it *means*.

EFFECTS VERSUS POV DEBATE

Some of the first drawings of the moth-plane, which flies through the Bismuth realm, included much of the final design. But they also revealed some directions to avoid. A moth, with a few shifts in detail, looks awfully like a fish, as shown in Figure A.9. And *fish-plane* just doesn't have the same ring.

Designers often must decide when to sacrifice production values for game play immediacy. Sometimes it's important to deliver whiz-bang effects via *cut scenes*, while other times it's crucial to maintain the player's *POV* (point of view, a consideration that a filmmaker has to keep in mind at all times). This either/or debate occurred regarding the flight of the moth-plane through space. The plane turned out so well that many wanted to see it in flight.

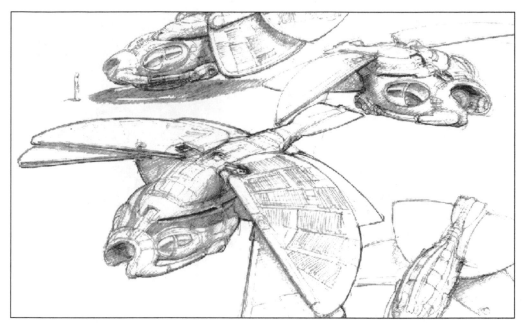

FIGURE A.9: Notice in this sketch of the moth-plane that its appearance resembles a fish.

Those on the other side of the debate wondered what the motivation was to create such a scene—since Lilah, or the player, was ensconced in the cockpit, sketched in Figure A.10.

In the end, it was time and budget again that led to the final decision. First-person POV may not be as flashy, but it sure is easier to create.

DREAM WORLD TRANSITION

One of the trickiest aspects of the *Obsidian* story was how to weave the theme of nano-technology throughout the game. It needed to be there from the beginning, subtly, so that as the truth behind the dream worlds became clear, the player would look back and realize that the pieces had been there all along.

Toward the end of the whole design process, a significant advance occurred. From the outset it was clear that when the player as Lilah was sucked inside the big black structure, some kind of special animation would happen. But what it would be, specifically, had never been worked out.

In one of their rambling design discussions—which usually start out with a roundup of current movies and proceed to possible restaurant choices for lunch and

FIGURE A.10: A third-person POV of Lilah, the player, behind the controls of the moth-plane once it has begun morphing into the Conductor realm.

then segue to office and family politics and then, having circled the inevitable for what seems like hours, finally land on the topic at hand (sort of like this sentence)—Adam Wolff and Howard Cushnir hit on the solution.

The nanobots would build the Bureau. (The Bureau used to be called the "Labyrinth," as you can see in the title to the early storyboard shown in Figure A.11.) This would be the animation that took the player from outside world to dream world. It would set the stage for everything to follow.

The style of the piece, which was doted over by art director Alex Laurent, borrowed heavily from a wonderful book called *Powers of Ten*. This book begins at the smallest microscopic level our current tools allow us to see, and then pulls back, over and over, until it ends at the largest possible view of the universe.

After the solution to this problem was discovered, it should be noted, Wolff and Cushnir then proceeded to argue, ad nauseam, over the relative merits of two take-out establishments until both such establishments had closed for the day and the possibility of lunch receded into distant memory.

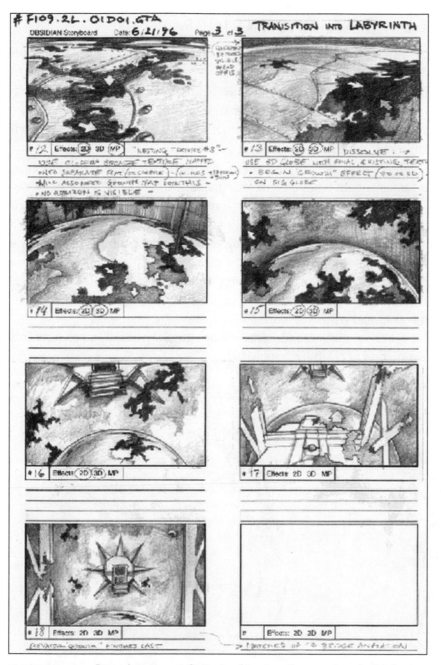

FIGURE A.11: Piece by piece, infinitesimal in size, the nanobots build the bureau.

THE SEQUEL TO WHICH ENDING?

With any luck, if you've finished *Obsidian,* you've had the chance to see both endings. Each has its own reward. The *win,* as it's referred to in the storyboard shown in Figure A.12 (although whichever ending the player chooses is truly the win), is exciting because of the implosion effect of the Conductor character.

The *lose* scenario, animated by Greg Gladstone, includes a flourish of his very own in which the Conductor *orchestrates* the world's devolution.

Notice the high heels in the storyboard (see Figure A.12). Each artist, it seems, has a particular fantasy about what a conscious machine might offer.

And here's an interesting riddle to ponder in regard to the sequel to *Obsidian.* If a game has two endings, and therefore two realities to leave the player with, how does a continuation of the story take both possible choices into effect? If it proceeds from the *win* scenario, then what does that say about the choice of the player who wanted to let Ceres complete its plan? Was the player wrong? And vice-versa, what if the sequel proceeds from the *lose* scenario? Then does that mean the player who saved our wretched Earth was mistaken?

Such are the conflicts inherent in interactive design. Stay tuned to see how this issue gets at least treated, if not fully resolved.

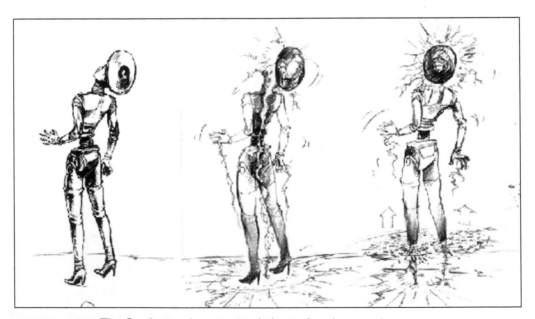

FIGURE A.12: The Conductor character implodes in the *win* scenario.

THE ROCK

The sketch of the big black rock shown in Figure A.13 is more jagged and scaly than the final choice. The look of the rock sets the stage for much of the game, and everyone labored over it for months.

Obsidian is both techno and organic, of course, and the problem was how much of either it should be. If it was too techno, Ceres's plan to remake the world at a cellular level would lose a little of its foreshadowing. If it was too organic, the structure wouldn't stand out enough from its surroundings.

At one point, in a scene from the game that didn't make the final cut, Max Powers talks about a combination of a spaceship and an organism. He calls it a "sporganism." This term, coined by Adam Wolff in one of his more delirious streams of consciousness, provided the tone for an effective blending of rock concepts.

One final thing to note about the structure: when you take the journey from tent to rock, on your way to being sucked in, it occurs in two different stages. First, the structure appears *comped in* to the real forest surrounding it. Then, as you get closer, the real environment disappears and the entire screen is computer-generated.

At its best, an effect like this is meant to be invisible. When you played through that section yourself, did you notice the transition taking place?

FIGURE A.13: This early rendering of the big black rock is more rugged and scaly than the final version.

CREDITS

ROCKET SCIENCE GAMES

Studio Creative Director	Bill Davis
Producer	Matthew Fassberg
Interactive Story & Design	Adam Wolff & Howard Cushnir and Scott Kim
Game Director	Adam Wolff
Lead Engineer	Andrew Rostaing

PRODUCTION TEAM

Production Supervision	Tom Laskawy
Engineering	Laurance Courdier
	Barry Gear
	Bruce Gottlieb
	Charlie Koehl
	Andrew Rostaing
CG Supervisor	Chris Hamilton
Art Direction	Alex Laurant
	Roy Forge Smith

Inspired by the Concepts and Artwork of Rich Cohen & Mark Sullivan with Additional Concepts by David Dodge

Production Design	Mark Nonnenmacher
	Honza Konopasek
	Jay Shuster

Additional Production Design	Erik Chan Cliff Iwai David Gordon
Character Design	Rich Cohen and Mark Sullivan
3-D Modeling	Erik Chan Brian Chee Wade Childress Rich Cohen Honza Konopasek Mark Nonnenmacher
Additional Modeling	George Chang Zygote Media Group
Digital Video	Chris Johnson Richard Young
Painters	Alan Sonneman Nicole McMath Mark Nonnenmacher Brian Flora Sara Simon
3-D Animators	David Brandt Richard McBride Etienne Jumelin Greg Gladstone Kathy O'Keefe Mark Powers

Additional Animators	Jong Yuk
	Gary Siela
	Erik Chan
	Cordt Holland
	Eli Delia
Digital Compositors	Wade Childress
	Chris Green
	Jance Allen
	David Dodge
	David Hoggan
	Colin Miller
	Joel Hornsby
	Richard McBride
	Josh Ferguson

Bismuth Realm Lighting and Animation by Pixel Liberation Front

PLF President	Colin Green
PLF Animators	John Vegher
	Scott Sindorf
	Peter Oberdorfer
	Mike Schmitt
PLF Coordinator	Susan Colletta
Additional Animation by	Moving Media—Fred Lewis
	Little Fluffy Clouds—Betsy De Fries,
	Jerry van de Beek
Interface Design	Robert Gagnon
File Puzzle Illustrations	All-Star Pictures

Music and Sound by	Thomas Dolby & Headspace
Headspace Production Manager	Mary Coller
Composers	Blake Leyh Thomas Dolby Kim Cascone Paul Sebastian
Sound Design	Blake Leyh
Sound Editor	Kim Cascone
Voice Over Recorded at	Hadley Sound
Stock Footage	Energy Productions, Inc. Archive Films, Inc.
An Extra Special Thanks to	Bryn Dyment and mFactory Engineering
Asset Coordinators	Josh Ferguson Heather Field
Asset Processing	Deb Asch Pam Fusco Gina Trbovich
QA Manager	Tony Ciarrocchi
QA Lead/Spider QA Lead	Billy Davis
QA Assistant Lead/Bureau QA	Lead Ivan Foong
Bismuth QA Lead	Heather Meigs

Forest QA Lead	William Sudderth
Conductor QA Lead	David Schultz
QA Technicians	Rich Montgomery
	Jim Chan
	Jamal Jennings
	Ben Davis
	Sean McGrath
	Roy Oakes
	Leah Beth Tomanek
	Eric Moser
Casting	Meryl Shaw

CAST

Max	Peter Callender
Lilah	Emilie Talbot
Young Max	Kennard Love
Conductor Voice	Susan Jerome
School Teacher	Robin Fernandez
Vidbots	Wade Childress
	Howard Cushnir
	Jym Dingler
	Matthew Fassberg
	Heather Field
	Pam Fusco
	J.S. Gilbert
	Scott Kim
	Peggy Koorhan
	Tom Laskawy
	Blake Leyh
	Lani Minella
	Veronica O'Donovan

Andrew Rostaing
Roy Smith
Gina Trbovich
Adam Wolff

LIVE ACTION

Producer	Eden Johnson
Director	Howard Cushnir
Videographer	Lou Weinert
Steadicam Operator	Gavin Eames
Property Master	Garren Bouget
Gaffer	Leo Nash
Wardrobe	Debra Dapolito
Production Assistant	Mark Eisenberg

Director of Production Services	Susanna Richards
Director of Game Engineering	Evan Robinson
Blue Screen Stages Provided by	Golden Gate Studios
	Pacific Video Resources
Masseuse	Erica Essner

SPECIAL THANKS TO: Darren Atherton, Ay Chihuahua, Peter Barrett, Steve Blank, Richard Booroojian, Hugh Bowen, Mark Brutten, Greg Butler, Cathy Callahan, Sean Callahan, Aaron Callanta, Sue Clark, Ron Cobb, Dave Chang, D. Michael Edgar, Paul Gluck, Purple Hampton, Ed Harp, Tom Hays, Kim Hilquist, Dan Irish, Julie Jaros, Jill Keith, Ryan Kellogg, Vicki Knapp, Lee Kramer, Mark Krueger, Lee Montgomery, Desmond Mullen, Mark Mullen, Tony Myles,

Dave Nakabayashi, Molly Naughton, Leah Nelson, Jim Noonan, Mike O'Donnell, Veronica O'Donovan, William Opdyke, Greg Orr, J Patton, Pepitos Parrilla, Pier 40, Primo Patio, MeMe Rasmussen, Sara Reeder, Stephen Rodriguez, Tony Ruffo, Bob Salera, Keith Schaefer, Dave Siegel, South Beach Cafe, TC's Cafe, Dave Theurer, Karen Toronjo, U.S. Park Service, Rob Vedovi, Jeffery Ventrella, Josh Viers, Jim Wickett, Brandy Wilson.

SPECIAL SPECIAL THANKS TO: Steve Blank, who kept the lights on for three, years.

EXTRA SPECIAL THANKS TO: Imperial Bank (especially Sam Bhaumik), SegaSoft, Mondadori, Gray Cary Ware & Freidenrich (especially Brad Rock), and our Venture Capitalists: Merill Pickard, Anderson, Eyre, And Mohr Davidow Ventures III.

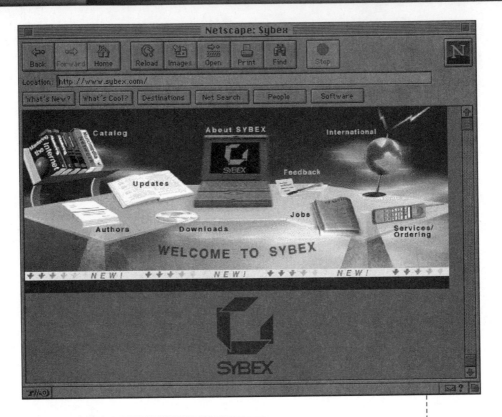